# HIGH SPIRITS

# HIGH SPIRITS

## Joan Sims

**CORGI BOOKS**

**HIGH SPIRITS**
**A CORGI BOOK : 0 552 14763 X**

Originally published in Great Britain by Partridge,
a division of Transworld Publishers

PRINTING HISTORY
Partridge edition published 2000
Corgi edition published 2001

1 3 5 7 9 10 8 6 4 2

Set in 11/13pt Sabon by
Falcon Oast Graphic Art.

Corgi Books are published by Transworld Publishers,
61–63 Uxbridge Road, London W5 5SA,
a division of The Random House Group Ltd,
in Australia by Random House Australia (Pty) Ltd,
20 Alfred Street, Milsons Point, Sydney, NSW 2061, Australia,
in New Zealand by Random House New Zealand Ltd,
18 Poland Road, Glenfield, Auckland 10, New Zealand
and in South Africa by Random House (Pty) Ltd,
Endulini, 5a Jubilee Road, Parktown 2193, South Africa.

Printed and bound in Great Britain by
Cox & Wyman, Reading, Berkshire.

# Contents

# Copyright Acknowledgements

Excerpts from *Carry On Up the Khyber*, *Carry On Up the Jungle* and *Carry On – Don't Lose Your Head* © and reproduced courtesy of Carlton International Media Ltd

Excerpts from *Carry On Cowboy*, *Carry On Teacher* and *Carry on Regardless* © Canal + Image UK Ltd

Excerpt from *Doctor in the House* © and reproduced courtesy of Carlton International Media Ltd

Lyrics from 'Oh Not Again, Ken', 'Hurry Up, Gran', 'Spring Song' and 'Men' by Ted Dicks and Myles Rudge © 1963 Tro Essex Music Ltd of Suite 2.07 Plaza Kings Road, London SW10 0SZ. International copyright secured. All rights reserved. Used by permission.

Lyrics from *Instant Marriage* by Bob Grant © and reproduced by kind permission of Movie Music Ltd

Excerpt from *The Cobblers of Umbridge* © John Wells and John Fortune

'The Ballad of Basher Green' reproduced by permission of Ronnie Cass

# Opening Credits

Unlike many who have lived their lives in the acting profession, I have kept precious little by way of a record of my career. Around my flat there are a few souvenirs – such as my graduation certificate from RADA, a framed photo of Hattie Jacques, an inscribed plate from Kenneth Williams and two little polished wooden boxes from Ronnie Barker, the exact nature of which you will read about later in these pages – but I have never made any systematic attempt to maintain a detailed chronicle.

Consequently I have had to enlist the help of various friends in order to create *High Spirits* – the title of this book is borrowed from one of my favourite revues of the 1950s – and I'd like to start by thanking those who have jogged my memory or tried (not always successfully) to help me fill in the gaps, notably Myles Rudge, Ronnie and Valerie Cass, Bob and Trisha Larbey, Pat Clayfield, Eleanor Fazan ('Fiz'), Norah Holland, Jack and Elsa Dean, Ronnie Barker, Elsie Weedon, Laurena Dewar, Audrey Ladbrook, Sean Magee and Richard Hatton.

# 1

# The Railway Child

When I was young, the height of my ambition was to be a thoroughgoing *femme fatale*.
　Or, to put it another way:

When I was young the height of my ambition
Was to be a thoroughgoing *femme fatale*:
I wanted to lure men into positions
Where they'd gladly offer me the Taj Mahal.
Alas, among life's flurry and its hubbub
My great ambition seemed to drift away;
Now I'm working on a station in a subbub,
Announcing train arrivals every day.
But still I think of what I'd be if I could have the
　choice
And my frustrated sex appeal just creeps into my
　voice:

When I say [*very huskily:*] 'Woking . . . Woking . . .'
It's thoroughly provoking for the men who travel
　up from Platform Two

11

I just say 'This is Woking'
And the thoughts that I'm evoking
Keep them panting till they get to Waterloo.
It's more the way I say it than the actual things I
    say
They may be great big businessmen but in my
    hands they're clay
That's why city gents all faint when I say,
    'There's a slight delay . . .'
They're the victims of the golden voice.

'Siren Song', one of my big numbers in the 1954 revue *Intimacy at 8.30*, was a sort of mini-autobiography in itself. For although the stage was not in my blood, railways certainly were.

I was born Irene Joan Marion Sims on 9 May 1930 in the station house at Laindon, Essex, where my father was station master. Laindon has now been swallowed up by the expansion of Basildon New Town, but then it was a little community on its own, a stop on the Shoeburyness to Fenchurch Street line which every day carried thousands of Essex commuters into and out of central London; a magical world full of those wonderful old steam engines thundering through and wagons shunting in and out of the goods yard.

Both my parents were Essex born and bred.

My father John Henry Sims – usually known as John, but sometimes as Harry – came from Grays, and had joined the London, Midland and Scottish Railway (LMS) as a booking clerk on being demobbed from the City of London Regiment at the end of the First World War. After serving in Malta and seeing action in the trenches he had suffered shell shock, and although he never mentioned his wartime experiences to me, I'm sure they affected him for the rest of his life: nowadays he'd have had proper psychiatric treatment, but back then it was not something you talked about – at least not in our household. Good-looking, tall and erect, with deep blue eyes, he was always turned out immaculately while on duty as station master, right down to the pair of kid gloves which he invariably carried.

My mother Gladys, ten years younger than my father, was a very attractive lady with dark chestnut hair. She came from Great Wakering, near Southend, and was hugely proud (as were we all) of her family's connection with royalty: her brother George Ladbrook was driver to the Duke of Windsor, who had abdicated as King Edward VIII in 1936 to be succeeded by his brother. One of my earliest memories is of going to visit my uncle when he was working for the then Prince of Wales at Marlborough House in The Mall, and seeing the elderly Queen Mary sitting in the summer-house in the garden. Working for royalty had its perks, and in May 1937, a few days after my seventh birthday, my four cousins and I crammed on to the balcony of Marlborough House to watch the Coronation procession of George VI pass by – an experience which I found so thrilling that I wet my knickers and was forced to slip them off and hide them under the bath in the nearest bathroom. I wonder if they're still there . . .

Laindon station was quite a family affair, as Aunt Edith, my mother's younger sister, served in the sweet and tobacco kiosk on the up-line platform. But as an only child, with no siblings and to all intents and purposes no neighbours – the station house stood all by itself at the bottom of the approach road – I had to endure a rather lonely childhood, deprived for much of the time of the close company of other children. My only real friend at Laindon was the local grocer's daughter Joyce Spire, a few years older than me and known to me as 'Doyce' as I could not, with my infant tongue, pronounce her name correctly. It is little wonder that, thrown back upon my own vivid imagination, I soon got used to making my own entertainment.

From a very early age my great passion was performing. Inside the station house, I would spend hours preening myself in front of the long mirror in my parents' bedroom. The station offered a ready-made stage in the form of the loading bays in the goods yard: these faced directly towards the platforms, and there I found my first audience – the stream of passengers using the station every day, for whose amusement I would dress up, in anything from an eiderdown to whatever I could raid from my mother's wardrobe, and put on impromptu performances.

Laindon station was a world of its own, rich in characters.

There was Mr Gibbons the coal merchant, whose wonderful draught horses not only pulled his carts but also provided rich comic material for my father's imagination: his daft stories about how Mr Gibbons's horses would dress up in ball gowns and go to local dances, where they would dance together on their hind legs, kept me in stitches.

Then there was Peg Leg, an old boy whom the war had left with two wooden legs. He would take the up train into London in the morning and return late in the afternoon, very much the worse for wear. His routine became so well known at the other end that the station master at Fenchurch Street would phone down to Laindon to let my father know which train Peg Leg was on. Two of our porters would be waiting to meet that train with one of those two-wheeled luggage trolleys; the comatose Peg Leg would be lifted out of the carriage and on to the trolley and then wheeled all the way home, one porter pushing the trolley along while the other kept Peg Leg upright. You don't get service like that these days!

Before I was very old my performances started to get quite a following among the passengers, though their enthusiasm did not always meet with the approval of my parents, who were strongly of the opinion that little girls should be seen and not heard, and did not encourage such informal relations between the station master's daughter and the public. One old lady, Mrs Chester, came down to the station with her wind-up gramophone so that she and I could put on an impromptu musical show in the ladies' waiting room. But the melodies wafting along the platform did not appeal to my father. We heard a startled cry of 'What's that noise?' and in he came to call a halt to our entertainment with his usual order to me to stop what I was doing and go inside: 'Joan – doors!'

My obsession with dressing up was somewhat restricted by my mother's shoes being – unsurprisingly – rather too large for my little feet, but I soon found a way round this. From a very early age I had acute powers of observation, and among the regulars who came in and out of the station I had noticed a lady who came every evening to meet her husband off the London train: a lady with exceptionally small feet. I made a point of getting into conversation with her, and when I judged the time to be right made my proposition: If ever you have any old shoes you don't want, please could you let me have them for my dressing-up games? Just leave them care of the station master. A couple of days later she duly deposited a bag full of cast-off footwear at the office – but my father, feeling the dignity of his position was compromised by being used as a clearing house for second-hand shoes, was not pleased: 'Joan, I will not have you scrounging off the passengers – I really will not have this on my station.'

Nor was he amused whenever he caught me indulging in one of my very favourite pastimes – playing shove-ha'penny with the porters in their rest room. 'Joan – doors!' But more often than not the porters would be able to warn me that he was approaching: I'd scurry under the table, they'd swear I wasn't in there, and as soon as he'd gone we'd resume our game.

A potent symbol of the discipline my father expected to be preserved around the house was the cane which hung on the back of the kitchen door. I cannot recall its ever having been marshalled into service, but its very presence offended me, and one morning when I was about nine I went downstairs from my bedroom, took the cane down, broke it into three pieces and threw it on the fire. Nothing was said, but its absence must have been noted . . .

That cane was all part and parcel of my father's attitude not only to the running of Station House, but to the station itself. He was exceptionally proud of having won an award for the best railway station garden, so understandably he tried to discourage me from using the place as my personal adventure playground – though this did not prevent my regular visits down the line to the signal box, where I loved pulling the levers to change the signals (under strict supervision, you'll be relieved to hear).

Towards the end of the 1930s war was becoming inevitable, and the first indications of the impending change in the life of the station were beginning to appear. A sign reading 'IS YOUR JOURNEY REALLY NECESSARY?' was installed on the platform, and one day I spied a use for this. I had heard the expression 'five bob' and understood it to mean a reasonable sum of money, and I saw a way to make a few shillings for myself. Out came my small scooter, then my father's paint pots. I proceeded to paint the scooter brown all over – then turned round 'IS YOUR JOURNEY REALLY NECESSARY?' and painted on the reverse a sign reading: 'SCOOTER FOR SALE – FIVE BOB – APPLY STATION MASTER'S OFFICE.'

I waited expectantly for likely purchasers, but as luck would have it the first person to see the advert was my father. He hit the roof: if any of the inspectors saw that sign he'd lose his job on the spot, he said; so the scooter, resplendent in its fresh brown paint, was hastily withdrawn from sale and the sign turned round to resume its role of public exhortation.

It wasn't only my father who took a dim view of my over-friendly relations with staff and passengers, and I suppose you can sympathise with my mother's growing irritation at having to welcome passengers who'd missed their trains and had been invited by that nice little girl into the station house for tea and cake . . .

Absorbed as I was in performing to the passengers, I was never much of a girl for dolls, whose only attraction, it seemed to me, was that they could be used as props for some of my acting games. Doctor Sims, for example, would perform operations on the dolls by boring holes into their stomachs with screwdrivers filched from my father's toolbox.

Had the chance ever presented itself, I would happily have bored a hole into the stomach of Mr

Higby, headmaster of my first school – St John's, the private school in Billericay to which my parents, trying to find me a more refined education than they thought was available at the local primary, sent me. But there was nothing very refined about Mr Higby, a vicious and deeply unpleasant man whose idea of discipline was to accompany any telling-off with a sharp pinch of the arm – though a far worse punishment awaited my classmate Colin Blanks from Battles Bridge.

Colin's great importance in my life is that he was the first boy with whom I fell hopelessly in love. I must have been all of seven years old at the time but I had a deep crush on him – for which he paid a terrible price. We were mad keen on one another and word spread round our class like wildfire, which led to a fierce bout of taunting from our classmates.

The girls were the worst. 'Bet you won't kiss Colin in front of the class!' they goaded, and for a spirited girl like me there was only one response. 'Bet you I will!' – and as I was doing so the door of the classroom opened and our teacher came in. An exhibition of kissing in front of the class was not acceptable behaviour at St John's, and we were both told to report to Mr Higby.

First into the headmaster's study was me. I was trembling at the enormity of the punishment that Mr Higby was about to bring down upon me, but to my huge relief I got away with a severe ticking-off. As I left the room, Colin came in to meet his fate. I waited outside, and through the closed door heard Mr Higby order Colin to take his trousers down. Six of the best – and then poor Colin emerged, tears streaming down his face. When he saw me there waiting for him he stopped sniffling, brightened up and, taking my hand, whispered: 'Well, it was worth it!'

I wish there'd been a few more men like that in my life.

(Years later, on a television chat show, I told the story of how Colin had suffered for our love. A few days after that I received a letter from one of Colin's sons, who had seen the interview and suggested I get in touch and meet my first love again. I thought about it and decided against: it was a sweet memory, and better to leave it as that.)

Colin Blanks apart, the high point of my time at St John's was being awarded as a prize (though I can't remember what for) a little book entitled *The Lady in the Chimney Corner*, on the inside cover of which one of the teachers had inscribed a very sound piece of wisdom:

> Life is an echo, all comes back
> The good, the false and the true;
> So give of the best that you can give,
> And the best will come back to you.

They don't write 'em like that any more.

It was while I was at St John's that a boy named Harman took me on one side and gave me the benefit of his knowledge of the facts of life. What ladies and gentlemen got up to in order to produce babies did not figure at all on the agenda at the station house, so everything Harman had to impart was at first shocking and then profoundly puzzling. *You did what?* – it sounded highly improbable to me. I needed corroboration of Harman's account, so when I got home that afternoon I rushed in to where my mother was sitting sewing: 'Mummy, Mummy, guess what Harman told me!' – and out it all came. She was in no mood to elaborate on the details which Harman had furnished, but instead told my father, who told Miss Short the elocution teacher, who told Mr Higby.

There was a huge hoo-hah. For a while the threat of expulsion hung over the unfortunate Harman, but then he was let off with a very severe warning not to fill his schoolmates' minds full of such filth. The fuss died down, but I had learned something which I would never have been told at Station House.

I also went to the local Methodist Sunday School, though what was on offer there had little appeal for me – so little that one Sunday three of us bunked off and spent the morning knocking back Tizer on the local recreation ground. I would have got away with this sinful escapade had not the father of one of the other girls mentioned our little adventure to my father while they were having a pint at nearby Langdon Hill Bowls Club (where my father was one of the leading players). The casual revelation from his friend that 'my daughter had a bit of fun with your daughter the other day' did not go down well at Station House, and I was banished to my bedroom.

Being sent upstairs for some naughty deed or other was not an unusual occurrence, and in any case it was not much of a punishment for me, as it gave me the opportunity for yet another rummage through my mother's wardrobe in the search for fresh costumes.

For all the delights of make-believe, though, even in my early years I started to see the darker side of life.

When I was eight an old friend of my parents came to stay, and one afternoon he went out for a walk with my mother and myself. While out on the walk he complained of feeling ill, so my mother found a taxi to take us home – where the old man walked into the front room, sat down in a chair and promptly slumped forward. He was dead, and I stood there watching with fascination as his front teeth fell out and he urinated into his trousers. My mother rushed around phoning the police and the undertaker while I lurked in a corner of the room taking in all this panic and bedlam. When the police-man arrived it turned out to be the same officer who a few weeks earlier had been summoned by my father to tell me off for spending my school milk money on sweets, and although my mother wanted me to leave the room this policeman insisted that it would do me good to stay and watch. I did so, and even did my bit to help out, opening the door to the undertaker – whose awful bright red wig was for me the most upsetting part of the whole episode.

This was, of course, the era of steam trains, and I have another vivid memory of an engine driver being brought into the station house severely burned by steam. My mother covered him in flour until the ambulance came. It was typical of my mother that she knew exactly what to do in such circumstances, for although my father was the public side of the station, she was a very tough cookie in her own right and ran the household with a rigid efficiency. She was also very artistic in a practical sort of way, brilliant at crochet, the most delicate *petit point* and tatting – I still have two tablecloths, the tatting on which bears testament to her great skill; when she had time would devote hours to knitting and pottery, and she was a great gardener. More to the point as far as parental influence on my future career was concerned, she had a very good singing voice and was an accomplished pianist. When I was old enough I started having lessons with the local piano teacher, Miss Sparrow, and the station house would ring with the sound of me hammering out 'Au Clair de la Lune' on the black ebony upright. But although I loved playing I was too lazy to apply myself to practice and in due course dropped the lessons.

My father's musical talents did not stretch to the piano – he aspired no higher than the Jew's harp – but his love of radio, and especially of radio comedy, made its mark on me. Radio was my father's great relaxation when off duty, and even if we had company in the house I'd catch him bending his ear towards the trusty old Roberts in the

23

corner of the sitting room. He adored programmes such as *ITMA*, *Life with the Lyons* and *Workers' Playtime*, and he loved comedians like Robb Wilton, his laughter bordering on the hysterical when a joke hit a nerve – though my mother was less inclined to such raucousness, and I can still hear her primly saying to my dad after something had tickled his fancy: 'I don't know what you see to laugh about in that . . .'

Those radio programmes gave me an early education in how you can get people laughing by putting on funny voices, and I was soon adding my own impression of Mrs Mopp in *ITMA* ('Shall I do you now, sir?') to my goods-yard act. But it wasn't only comedy which caught my young imagination: radio programmes such as *The Man in Black* with Valentine Dyall had me gripped – and triggered in me a lifelong fascination with crime stories.

My mother was subject to occasional bouts of depression (though of course I did not recognise it as such at the time), and during one off these dark moods, when I was about nine, she decided that the time had come to tell me about the nature of my parents' marriage. It was one afternoon when we were together in the sitting room and my father was working outside on the station. She quietly took an old photograph from its hiding place at the back of the desk drawer. The photo was of a young man, and before I had a chance to ask my mother who it was she let me into her dark secret. Before she and my father had married she had been madly in love with another man, she told me tearfully, and expected that they would marry. He came from what she considered a better background than her – she was always rather sensitive about being from 'country folk' – and one day after she had suggested that she take him home to meet her parents she got cold feet, cancelling their arrangement and saying she couldn't see him that day after all. She then went out and played tennis, he saw her doing so and jumped to the wrong conclusion, and their relationship ended. John Sims, long an admirer of Gladys Ladbrook, had been waiting in the wings and now saw the chance to make his move. They married shortly afterwards, though my mother told me she practically had to be forced to go to the register office: she didn't want to marry my father, but went through with it.

A couple of weeks after the wedding, the other man got in touch with her. He wanted to see her again – he hadn't heard of the drastic step she'd taken after they had finished – and, unbeknown to my father, she went up to London to meet him. There he declared undying love: it had all been a terrible mistake, and he wanted her to marry him. She had to tell him it was too late.

So, at the tender age of nine I was being asked to come to terms with the fact that my mother had not wanted to marry my father, and had been living all these years thinking of what might have been with the other man. That life could be so bleak was a terribly difficult lesson to have to learn so early, and I suppose this revelation explains why I never once saw my parents holding hands – let alone going in for a quick kiss. The child they bred turned out to be very different: I've always been a very touchy-feely person.

With my mother, I never felt the spontaneous affection between parent and child which I grew to envy so much in other families. If she hugged me, it always felt like a hug of necessity, or of some perceived parental duty, rather than the genuine article. (Much later in life, I was talking to my mother over the phone from London and somehow got round to confessing to her that as a child I'd never felt she'd given me a real hug. The next time I drove down to Essex, there she was, standing at the door to greet me as I parked the car. As I walked up the path she said, 'Well, I suppose I'd better give my daughter a hug,' and came forward and put her arms around me. I'd never experienced anything like it. She felt completely frigid, her arms stiff and unyielding like the branches of a tree. It was as if she was recoiling from me, and before I could stop myself I found myself saying: 'If that's the best you can do, don't bother in the future.' Even then there was no reaction.)

It's hardly surprising that the absence of day-to-day affection between my mother and father sent me looking elsewhere for a model of married life, and soon after my mother had told me all about the other man, I found it. My mother had a great friend called Louie Ventrice, who lived with her parents nearby, and on one of our regular visits there for tea my mother and I walked into their living room to find Louie's elderly parents sitting at the table holding hands. They held hands all through tea, disengaging only to pick up a teacup or a piece of cake – after which they'd quietly take each other's hands again. I remember thinking: That's what I want my marriage to be like. Idealistic, I know, and doubtless pure fantasy, but I knew from that afternoon that I could never bear to be in a marriage where there was tension and rowing; and, having looked around me and seen any number of marriages go that way, perhaps my idealism has stood me in good stead . . .

There were other signs that all was not well with my parents' own marriage, though I was too immature to interpret them at the time. For one thing, we hardly ever went on holiday all together. My mother and I would go off for a couple of weeks in the summer to the Essex coast, or down to visit my mother's sister Florence – Aunt Floss – and her husband Uncle Cecil at Hove (where they had a car showroom), while my father would stay behind at Laindon, unwinding from the heavy responsibility of running the station by pottering about in the garden. He seemed to hate the disruption of travelling, though with the benefit of hindsight I'm sure his aversion to change must have had much to do with his shell shock.

Aunt Floss and Uncle Cecil's main home was Orchard House in Great Wakering, not far from Laindon, where Uncle Cecil ran a successful fruit business in addition to the car showroom at Hove. Perhaps I was subconsciously relieved to be getting away from the underlying tension of family life at the station house, but my visits to Orchard House were invariably wonderful, and since Aunt Floss and Uncle Cecil had no children of their own they tended to spoil all their nieces and nephews – Aunt Edith's children Yvonne and Michael as well as George Ladbrook's four offspring – something rotten.

With its acres of fruit trees and resident population of pigs, geese and turkeys, Orchard House was a magical place for a small child, and I spent many happy summers there. Scrumping was out, though. Cecil knew those orchards like the back of his hand, and although it was all right to pick up and eat windfalls, woe betide anyone who took an apple off the tree. 'Who's had an apple off that Worcester?' he would ask accusingly, and it baffled me how he knew. But he did.

I was staying at Orchard House at the beginning of September 1939, and on the fateful Sunday morning was in the kitchen with my cousins Noel and Pat (two of my uncle George Ladbrook's four children) helping Aunt Floss prepare lunch, when just before eleven o'clock Uncle Cecil came in and said we were all to stop what we were doing and listen to the radio. He switched on the set in the corner, and within a few moments Neville Chamberlain's voice came crackling across the room telling us that we were at war with Germany. The Prime Minister had scarcely finished speaking when the air-raid siren sounded. Although I had little idea of what it all meant, I knew that something very serious was about to happen, and, to the scorn of my cousins, burst into tears: I just wanted to get home to the station house.

For the first year or so of the war, hostilities seemed to have little effect on life in Laindon, though once rationing had taken effect my mother's housekeeping skills really came into their own. The most common operations had to be carefully planned, and making a Christmas cake, for example, was no longer simply a matter of going out and buying the necessary: to produce a decent cake, all the different ingredients had to be hoarded for months.

So my mother was distinctly unamused when, having been shown how to make mud pies by Joyce, I gaily walked into the kitchen one morning, announced, 'Mud pie, Mummy!' and deposited a beautifully constructed mud pie straight into the Christmas cake mix. 'Joan – upstairs!'

(After the war Joyce married and left Laindon to move to Oxford; here she became friendly with many of the artists in the company at the Oxford Playhouse, and on one of my visits there she took me backstage to met Ursula Howells and Donald Houston – a great thrill for a young girl beginning to get interested in the theatre.)

My parents were anxious that I should go to Brentwood County High School for Girls, about six miles away. This was easier said than done, as I had not exactly distinguished myself at St John's. So they asked a teacher friend, Teddy Daynes, to provide extra tuition, and with this help I managed to get a place at Brentwood.

Teachers leave a deep impression on their pupils, and it is tempting to try to connect some of the ladies who taught me at the Brentwood County High School for Girls with characters I played later.

There was Miss Hodge the English teacher, who used to ride to school on her bicycle with her white hair tied up in a bun. We played her up mercilessly, as her reaction was wonderful to behold. The usual trick was to throw the blackboard duster up over the light fitting before she arrived in our classroom and await her entrance.

'Good morning, girls! . . . Now, where is my duster?' – and when she found and retrieved it and had to confront our smirking faces, her reaction was always: 'Oh, you beauties, I wish I had a camera!'

(Years afterwards I heard that she had been knocked off her bicycle while cycling to school and killed.)

There was Miss Goodwin the PT instructor, doubtless a model for Miss Allcock in *Carry On Teacher*. Certainly Miss Allcock's walk in that film owed something to Miss Goodwin's gait – a sort of half run, half trot – and Miss Goodwin always had a whistle in her mouth ('Come along, girls! – one, two, three!'). She was not in the mould of the traditional hearty, thigh-slapping gym mistress, but had a certain sexiness which I'm sure I tried to recreate in Miss Allcock.

The maths mistress Miss Vasher-Bacon – we girls, with sparkling wit, used to call her Rasher

Bacon – was all haversack, sensible shoes, Bermuda shorts (even in class) and socks. She had a very close friendship with another teacher, Miss Whitehouse (we were too innocent to appreciate just *how* close), and a familiar sight after school on Friday afternoons was of the pair of them all kitted out and setting off on their weekend hike.

But the greatest influence on my life at this time was Miss Wilson, who taught elocution. To me she represented glamour: she was the one teacher at the school who wore red nail varnish and make-up, and she sported a wonderful oblong ring consisting of a large emerald surrounded by diamonds. So it was not just her subject which attracted me to Miss Wilson, though I had already undertaken some training in elocution at St John's (it's never too early to start dropping the flat vowels of the Essex accent) and to me an elocution lesson was a joy – the one lesson in which I didn't feel a failure.

For there was no getting away from it: I was considered a failure at school, and my reaction to constantly being told that I was not much good gradually grew into a determination to find something – *anything* – at which I could excel.

My school reports tended always to take the same line: Joan could be very good at this subject if only she would concentrate. Looking back on my inability to shine at school, I now wonder if I was dyslexic, since I had great difficulty sustaining my concentration when reading: I found myself going over the same word or line again and again, and soon the words would start jumping about in front of my eyes. No wonder I wasn't making the right sort of progress. At that time, though, teachers were not as sensitive to dyslexia as they are now, and it was assumed that I was just unable to keep my mind on the job.

On the other hand, I had no trouble concentrating every Saturday morning at Laindon's Radion Cinema, where Rita Hayworth and Betty Grable fuelled my dreams of becoming an actress, and Tyrone Power (of whom we shall be hearing more) stirred up other emotions. I have often been asked whether as a child I was stage-struck, whether visits to plays at an early age sparked a desire to become the next star of the West End theatre, and I have to admit that at that age watching live theatre – which meant the local repertory company, my sole early experience of the live stage – left me fairly cold. Certainly no great theatrical ambition was hatched at Westcliff-on-Sea rep.

Cinema, however, was a different matter altogether. I was besotted with the silver screen, and every Saturday at the Radion set my spine tingling and the hairs on the back of my neck standing up. Musicals had a special magic all of their own, and after gaping wide-eyed at the Ziegfeld Follies I'd skip down the steps of the cinema and *be* a Ziegfeld girl, dancing all the way back to Station House in my fantasy world. The fantasy faded, of course – it always does – and

Monday would bring the boring reality of having to go back to school.

Going to school in wartime had its distractions, however, and often our lessons at Brentwood would be interrupted by air raids, which would send us scuttling down into one of the school's Anderson shelters. In we filed, through the piece of sacking that hung across the entrance doorway, to sit on seats down either side of the long, half-buried shelter. At the other end another piece of sacking concealed the chemical toilet, and I soon discovered that the toilet seat made a wonderful drum for the little impromptu entertainments which we would stage to keep ourselves from being frightened by the bombs falling (or not) out-side. My classmate Margaret Holt specialised in singing Carmen Miranda-style samba tunes while I accompanied her on my makeshift drum – which was usually a signal for dear Miss Hodge to appear: 'Ooh, you beauties, I wish I had a camera! – But come along, girls, we must settle down and get on with our lessons.' I thought of my drum-ming as entertainment for the troops to keep their minds off the war, but Miss Hodge never quite saw it in the same way.

At Laindon Station the war made a more serious impact. Although three of my cousins – Audrey, Geoff and Pat – were evacuated to Minehead, I did not have to go through that painful separation from parents and home, and got used to going down into the station shelter with my mother as German bombers passed overhead, using the railway lines as their guide towards central London. If there was no time to get to the shelter, we'd huddle under the stairs in the house.

While we were not exactly in the front line, I experienced the war at closer hand than most young children. Since the railways attracted enemy bombers, an anti-aircraft gun was installed in the goods yard. My father must have forgotten to warn me about this, as the first time the gun sent a burst of fire after an enemy bomber the racket scared the living daylights out of me. We were always finding shrapnel in the goods yard, too. And on one occasion I vividly recall standing on the highly polished Victorian lavatory seat in the station house and stealing a look out of the tiny window on to the platform where a train carrying a group of German prisoners had just come in. The prisoners were on their way to the nearby camp at Langdon Hills, and there was my father, immaculately turned out as ever from his station master's cap to his highly polished shoes, striding up and down the platform calling out what seemed to me to be 'Oust! Oust!' – but was in fact ''Raus!', the German for 'Get out!' He seemed to have taken on a completely different personality, but in view of what happened to him in the First World War it's hardly surprising that he had deep feelings about Germans.

My family, like so many, had its own wartime tragedy. I was devoted to my older cousin Noel, and drooled when I saw him in his Air Force uniform: he looked so handsome. Noel joined the

Coastal Command, and flying back from an operation one night his plane flew into a snow-storm and crashed into a hill. There were no survivors.

It was during this period that I had what might be called my first 'official' acting role, as the St John Ambulance brigade staged regular practice sessions at the station, and I volunteered to act as a wounded casualty. But my greatest source of pride was my appointment as leader of the Blue Tit Patrol of the local company of Girl Guides. (Years later I told Ronnie Barker that I had been leader of the Blue Tit Patrol. 'A very wise choice,' he said.) It was a bitterly cold day when I achieved this accolade, but I walked home up the approach road to the station and over the footbridge to our house without wearing my coat, so keen was I to show off my newly won lanyard to the people of Laindon. Throughout my childhood I loved wear-ing uniforms (no doubt preparing myself for the versions worn by Nurse Stella Dawson, Policewoman Gloria Passworthy, etc.), and found group activities such as the Girl Guides and the Girls Training Corps a welcome antidote to the isolation of life at Station House.

I was fifteen when the war ended, and spent VJ night in August 1945 down in Hove, where Uncle Cecil and Aunt Floss had a flat above the car showroom.

The party atmosphere that evening was wonder-ful, made all the more so by my friend Doris and I hitching up with a couple of young Canadian Air

Force boys. Mine – a real dreamboat with a lovely face, flaming auburn hair and, most alluring of all, a uniform – was called Red. As we danced the night away, I felt I was fulfilling all those Hollywood fantasies I'd started having at the Radion: I was Betty Grable, he was Tyrone Power. I didn't want the night to end. It had to, of course, and I never saw Red again – but we remained pen pals for quite a while after he returned to Canada.

It was in my early teens that I started to get seriously interested in drama, hoping to make something of those energies with which I had tried to entertain the local commuters over the years, and joined the local amateur dramatic society, the Langdon Players. Having spent the previous decade learning how to work an audience from the improvised platform of the goods yard, I took to a more orthodox stage like a duck to water, and loved every second of every production – though even at that tender age I seemed to be typecast as a lady of considerable age and few teeth, in roles like Madame Arcati in Noël Coward's *Blithe Spirit* or the mother-in-law in his *Fumed Oak*. (During one performance I heard a lady in the front row saying to her neighbour: 'Surely she hasn't got her teeth out at her age . . .')

I also joined the local operatic society – whose repertoire was confined to Gilbert and Sullivan operettas such as *The Mikado* or *The Gondoliers* – as well as doing as much acting as I could for the Youth Centre. Drama apart, the great attraction of the Youth Centre for me was the dancing instructor, Frank Gammon, on whom I developed a mad crush. He wore a bright white mac, which served as a sort of early-warning system for my over-protective mother on the nights he walked me home: halfway down the approach road I could see the curtains in the station house twitching.

In 1946 the Youth Centre Drama Group entered the South East Essex Drama Festival at Walthamstow with a short play called *Lonesome Like*, a four-hander set in industrial Lancashire, with Miss Joan Sims in the role of a mill hand. The main adjudicator was the famous writer and critic L. A. G. Strong, and although our production did not get among the prizes, my own performance won the Palm of the Day for Best Individual Performance of the Festival. I was thrilled – here at last was recognition that I was good at something I enjoyed doing. More than that: beyond the immediate euphoria, the award meant that I was now in a position to take my acting seriously, even to the point of considering the stage as a career. It was time for some decisions.

Brentwood County High School had not turned me into an academic star. My first attempt at School Certificate – the equivalent of today's GCSEs – had come to grief as I'd failed in one of the five subjects I'd sat. (I was good at English, art and domestic science but fairly useless at maths and science.) My next attempt went pretty much the same way. Having failed School Certificate twice, as I approached the end of my time at school the career options seemed limited. My father was keen that I should follow him into the railways by training to become an interior designer working in railway hotels, whereas my mother thought a clerical job would be nice and respectable, and one day took me up to London to visit a friend who worked in a large insurance company to see about the employment prospects there. I was taken to see the typing pool to encourage me towards my mother's way of thinking, but the grim sight of row upon row of young girls, all manically typing away as if their lives depended on it, had entirely the opposite effect. Office life was definitely not for me.

The Palm for Best Performance at the South East Essex Drama Festival may not have been an Oscar, but it pushed ajar a door that I was mad keen to go through, and I found two useful allies in the shape of my elocution teacher Miss Wilson and the warden of the Youth Centre, Mr Hill. They had both seen my acting talent and were determined that I should develop it. Miss Wilson managed to convince my parents of this, which took some doing – though, to be fair, their scepticism was based less on hostility towards the theatrical profession than on simple ignorance of it. Although they would come and see me in local amateur productions, the professional theatre was a completely alien world to them.

As far as my parents were concerned, if I was adamant that I wanted to try to get into the theatre they would go along with the idea, but I had to have a proper training. Drama school was expensive, and there was no possibility whatever of their being able to afford it, so Miss Wilson and Mr Hill contacted the Essex Education Committee to enquire about a grant. I was told that the Committee would finance me if I could get a place at RADA, the Central School of Speech and Drama or the Young Vic. My first choice was RADA – the august Royal Academy of Dramatic Art in Bloomsbury – and I duly took the up train to London and made my way to Gower Street for my first serious brush with what has remained the bane of my acting life ever since: the audition.

I was shown into a bleak, bare rehearsal room, and there confronted with a panel of the six people – including, I later discovered, the great actress Athene Seyler – who would decide my future. I offered them two readings, strongly contrasting in nature. The first was the episode from *Winnie-the-Pooh* In Which Eeyore Loses A Tail And Pooh Finds One, which offered a great opportunity for different voices:

And the door opened, and Owl looked out.

'Hallo, Pooh,' he said. 'How's things?'

'Terrible and sad,' said Pooh, 'because Eeyore, who is a friend of mine, has lost his tail. And he's Moping about it. So could you very kindly tell me how to find it for him?'

'Well,' said Owl, 'the customary procedure in such cases is as follows.'

'What does Crustimoney Proseedcake mean?'

39

said Pooh. 'For I am a Bear of Very Little Brain, and long words Bother me.'

'It means the Thing to Do.' . . .

Having captivated them (as I hoped) with that, I proceeded to tug at their heart-strings (as I hoped) with the trial scene from Shaw's *Saint Joan* ('They told me you were fools, and that I was not to listen to your fine words nor trust to your charity . . .').

Thank you, we'll let you know – and as I left the room I passed the next poor devil going in.

As the train rattled back to Laindon I stared out of the window and thought over the day. My choice of material for the audition had been ridiculous, and had clearly not gone down well with the panel. (Years later Athene Seyler confided to me that she was put off me as she couldn't abide A. A. Milne.) But I couldn't blame my pessimism purely on the choice of pieces I had read. Was there some deeper problem? Did I *really* want to be an actress, or was I just following this course as part of my general obsession with finding some activity at which I could excel? If so, was that enough?

Sure enough, the letter marked 'Royal Academy of Dramatic Art' which was eventually delivered to the station house told me that I had failed to get in.

This was a blow, but the rejection letter contained a considerable crumb of comfort: although I had not scored sufficient marks to gain a place at RADA straight away, it was recommended that I spend a period at the preliminary academy, PARADA, and try again for RADA proper the following term. So they must have recognised some talent in me, I thought, and, having received the go-ahead from the Essex Education Committee, I enrolled at PARADA early in 1947.

The training provided at RADA's prep school – situated on Shepherd's Hill in Highgate, north London – was a sort of junior version of what awaited those who went on to 'the big school', with much of our time taken up by classes in such skills as elocution, mime, fencing (yes, fencing, even for the girl students) and diction. But the formal education was only part of the influence PARADA was to exert on my acting life. Far more important were the people I met there, many of whom have remained friends to this day. There was Myles Rudge, with whom I would later work on all sorts of shows and who wrote many songs for me; Ronnie Stevens, who years later would act alongside me in revue; and Pat Hornsby (now Pat Clayfield), who eventually gave up her acting career but is still one of my closest friends. I continued to live at Laindon, commuting every day to Highgate, but to find myself sharing a student existence with such a lively and varied group of fellow aspiring actors was a highly liberating experience.

In due course it was time for my second audition at RADA itself. I decided to ditch *Winnie-the-Pooh* in favour of more grown-up material and felt that I had put up a much better performance than on my first attempt. Since RADA had been so encouraging in recommending me to attend

PARADA, and since I felt I had on this occasion auditioned well, I was fairly confident that this time I would get in.

It was Christmas Eve 1947 when the letter arrived. I picked it out of the flurry of Christmas cards on the doormat at Station House and, trying to control my anxiety, walked with as much dignity as I could muster down to the far end of the goods yard, where I nervously tore open the envelope – and felt my world grind to a halt:

Dear Miss Sims

We regret to tell you that you have not secured sufficient marks for a place at RADA.

We would seriously advise you to discontinue your training as we feel you are quite unsuitable for the profession.

42

# 2

## Pick Yourself Up

When your chin is on the ground – according to that song I'd heard on old Mrs Chester's gramophone in the station waiting room – you pick yourself up, dust yourself off, start all over again.

But for me it wasn't quite that straightforward.

I had failed academically, and now I had learned that I was also officially useless at my one great passion and my greatest hope for the future. It wasn't that I was fired with a burning desire to emulate a particular role model – it was not a case of *who* rather than what do I *want* to be when I grow up; nor was I imbued with a fierce desire to be an actress. It was simply that I wanted to unearth something that I would be good at, and here I was confronted with the awful reality that acting was not, after all, that something. Palm of the Day for Best Individual Performance at the South East Essex Drama Festival was about as far as I was going to get. I'd better work out what I was going to do with the rest of my life.

More urgently, I had to tell my parents that my theatrical ambitions had been strangled at birth. I plucked up the courage, walked miserably back to the station house, and broke the news.

To my great relief, since I was well aware that they had been less than a hundred per cent enthusiastic about my passion for the stage, they were both extremely sympathetic and supportive – and my father, ever the man of action, decided that he'd do something about the situation.

A couple of days later Sir Kenneth Barnes, principal of RADA, received a letter from the father of one disappointed applicant asking, ever so politely, that she be given another chance to show her worth: she gets very bad nerves, the letter stressed, so would not show her true ability at an audition – and to press home just how good an actress his daughter was, my father had enclosed cuttings of reviews from the local papers.

It may have been a long shot but it did the trick. Back came a reply from Sir Kenneth, to the effect that it was admittedly difficult for the panel to base their decisions purely on a brief audition; and, given my stage experience and my ambition to make my way in the theatre, I could return to PARADA for an extra term with a view to auditioning again for RADA at the end of it. This was a lifeline. I grabbed it – thanks to the continuing support of the ever-patient Essex Education Committee – and returned to Highgate full of hope.

At the end of that term I presented myself yet

44

again for my audition to RADA. Third time lucky? Not quite – once more I had failed to get enough marks and was turned down. I could have been forgiven for feeling rather fed up with the whole business, but the suggestion that I stay on at PARADA for a third term was a pretty sure sign that they had it in mind to admit me to RADA eventually, and at the end of that third term I did indeed audition to their satisfaction. I was in – and a few weeks later presented myself at the reception of that anonymous building on Gower Street above the door of which was engraved in stone the magic name: The Royal Academy of Dramatic Art.

I had spent long enough at PARADA to have a head start in areas such as movement, ballet, voice production and diction – and, of course, I was a dab hand at fencing; so now I tried to concentrate on polishing the basics of stagecraft: how to work with props, how not to bump into people on stage, which hand to use when opening a door, and a hundred other tricks of the acting trade. But, as at the preliminary academy, the true education came not from the formal classes but from working with my fellow students.

They turned out to be a pretty distinguished lot. Dorothy Tutin, one of the greatest actresses of the modern age, was there, as were other performers I've long admired in Ian Holm, Barbara Jefford and Rachel Roberts; also Lynne Reid Banks, who would make her name as the author of *The L-Shaped Room*. Pat Hornsby, my old friend from PARADA, had moved on to RADA, as had Myles

45

Rudge and Ronnie Stevens. The male contingent also included Brian Matthew, soon to achieve fame as one of the country's favourite broadcasters but in those days with his sights set firmly on a stage career, and several students who went on to distinguish themselves in the theatre and television, including David Morrell (my first serious boyfriend), Derek Royle (my second), Ronald Lewis and Jimmy Grout, who late in his career became a familiar television presence in the character of Inspector Morse's boss. There was also a young man named Eric Taylor, who became a household name as Shaw Taylor, presenter of the pioneering crime-solving programme *Police Five*.

The focal points of study at RADA were the productions we put on at the end of term, a variety of works which provided experience in a wide range of theatrical styles. At the core of the selection, understandably, was Shakespeare; but although I did my bit in various plays – including Queen Margaret in *Richard III*, and Tranio in *The Taming of the Shrew* as there were not enough men to go round – I never really relished playing The Bard. Indeed, I spent a good deal of my early time at RADA never being quite clear whether this William Shakespeare fellow had been a real person or some fantasy figure.

If student life in Highgate had been a release from the constraints of Laindon, an even greater feeling of liberation came with the delights of central London and RADA: at last I was in the company of people with whom I shared a common passion for performing, and there was none of the feeling of inferiority I had endured at school alongside my more scholastically gifted classmates. I was in my element, and never more happy than when messing about – in the most innocent way imaginable – in a foursome with Pat Hornsby, Derek Royle and Brian Matthew: the summer's day when we went to Windsor and found the River Thames so inviting that we all stripped down to our underwear and dived in felt like a symbol of my new-found freedom.

I was not entirely at liberty to behave as I might have wanted, however, since I was still living at the station house at Laindon, and on one occasion my London social life was interrupted in a rather unexpected way. After our day's work a group of us were unwinding in the local corner café. I was sitting on David Morrell's knee when I happened to look up, into the mirror above the counter – and saw a very familiar figure approaching the door of the café. It was my father, up in London for the day on railway business. In he came, and with a cheery 'Hallo, Joan, I've come to take you home', whisked me away.

At least he didn't issue the old command: 'Joan – doors!'

That sort of parental presence was fairly restricting, and after I had been at RADA a while I pleaded with my mother and father to allow me to stay overnight in London one weekend for a party held by my friend Mary Neelands. The morning after that party I almost wished they had forbidden me to go, as it turned out to be the first time I ever got drunk. Alcohol did not feature in life at Station House – there was a bottle of sherry which spent most of the year gathering dust in the sideboard and would be brought out at Christmas, but that was about it – so I had very little idea of what drink could do to you.

Mary's party was an extremely merry gathering, with plenty of young men recently out of the forces making up for lost time, and when Eric Taylor offered me a paper cone containing an orange drink I drank it straight down. It tasted pretty good, so a few moments later I knocked back another, and it was then that I started to feel strange. As the evening went on I felt even stranger. The room started swaying, and then someone pointed out that what I had been imbibing so merrily was rum and orange. By then it was too late to prevent the inevitable consequences, and I spent the whole night hunched over the toilet bowl. I was throwing up so frequently and so violently that I didn't get the opportunity to go to bed at all, and spent the train journey back to Laindon the following day sitting on my pyjamas to make it appear to my mother that I had slept in them.

Making sure that my parents had no evidence of their daughter's first hangover tested my blossoming acting skills to the limit. In fact, those skills were being developed from within me much more than from watching contemporary performers in action. While in London I hardly ever went either to the theatre – it just didn't occur to me that I might learn something from seeing one of the greats, such as Edith Evans, on the stage – or even to the cinema. After the working day I'd simply catch the train back to Laindon, have supper and get ready for the next morning.

The Essex Education Committee had valiantly carried on supporting me, but any money I could earn to supplement my grant could always be put to good use, and one summer holiday I took a job as a sales assistant at the C&A department store in Oxford Street, an experience which provided endless material for future acting roles. It was the time of the summer sale, and I was sent to help out in the ladies' dresses department. Complete mayhem. It was like a rugby match, a mass of hot sweaty bodies charging around and pushing each other out of the way as ladies of every age, shape and girth fought madly among themselves to get the best bargains. (One lady was so appreciative of my help in finding her just the thing she was rummaging for that she offered me a tip, which, the shop's rules being strictly applied, I had to decline.)

A more congenial holiday job was as assistant stage manager in the repertory theatre at Southchurch, near Southend, which was near enough to Laindon to make it possible for me to continue to live at home. As well as the usual dogsbody ASM duties, one play brought me a slightly more unusual task. The case included an absolute heart-throb of a young actor – tall, svelte, masses of dark hair – playing an American army sergeant. The plot demanded he make a very quick change of costume between appearances on stage, and my job was to stand in the wings and rip his clothes off as he made his exit – to think I was being paid for doing that! – and then rapidly help him into his next costume. I was soon nurturing a deep crush on him, though sadly nothing came of it. This gorgeous young actor's name was Stratford Johns, destined to make his name as Chief Inspector Barlow in *Z Cars* – and by the time, many years later, that I recalled his period at Southchurch rep on his *This Is Your Life*, not much of that flowing hair was still in evidence.

Back at RADA, I was enjoying myself, but as the end of my two years there approached early in 1950, I can't honestly say that I was bursting to get out into the world and knock 'em dead as the new Ginger Rogers. Beyond wanting to work to earn the money which would bring independence, and wanting to prove to myself (and, I suppose, to my parents) that I could do something more than sit in the typing pool, I had no particular goal.

I graduated from RADA on 4 April 1950, five weeks short of my twentieth birthday. The traditional final fling of each year's departing contingent was the Public Show, a 'showcase' production at Her Majesty's Theatre in the West End where the students would display their skills to an audience which always included agents on the lookout for fresh talent.

The initial idea of the Public Show committee was that I should play Abraham Lincoln's wife in one of the showcase pieces, but that idea was soon squashed: some people can't see beyond the end of their own noses, and I was not considered posh enough for a serious role, being thought of, even then, as 'a bit too musical comedy'. So I was switched to another wifely role – in a dance drama which chronicled how Henry VIII disposed of his various consorts (and thus a premonition of one of my favourite *Carry On* incarnations years later): the piece, completely without dialogue, was played in period costume but was hardly the ideal vehicle for presenting my acting skills to all those agents and producers in the audience.

A few days after the production came the prize-giving, and we all took our seats in the auditorium as the bigwigs gathered on stage for the presentation ceremony. Sir Kenneth Barnes was sitting there with his devoted golden spaniel Marsha lying in front of him, and next to him sat one of my acting heroines, Margaret Leighton, who would be presenting the prizes. After everyone settled down, the announcement of the winners began.

The gold medal went to Brewster Mason. The silver medal went to Peter Fawcett. The list went on and on, with the name Joan Sims conspicuous – at least to me – by its absence. Before long there was only one more prize to award.

'And the ten-pound Mabel Temperley Prize for Grace and Charm of Movement goes to . . . Joan Sims.'

Palm of the Day for Best Performance at the

South East Essex Drama Festival, and now the ten-pound Mabel Temperley Prize for Grace and Charm of Movement! Surely an Oscar was only a matter of time.

As I proudly made my way up on to the stage to collect my tenner I maintained a suitably dignified bearing to match the award I had just won. Margaret Leighton graciously shook my hand and presented me with my envelope ('Many congratulations – I quite agree with the decision') – and I turned serenely to return to my seat. But this was too good a comic opportunity to miss, and as I reached the top of the stairs leading off the stage I deliberately missed my footing and went through the whole comedy trip-down-the-steps routine.

Sir Kenneth sprang to my aid with an anguished 'Are you all right, my dear?!' Marsha went berserk and started running up and down the stage yapping, and all the dignitaries rushed forward to help. I regained my balance and my composure and returned to my seat, to the vast amusement of my fellow students, who had quickly latched on to what I was doing.

(When years later I told Kenneth Williams that I had been the proud winner of the ten-pound Mabel Temperley Prize for Grace and Charm of Movement, his reaction was Kenny to the core: 'Hmmmm, that sounds a bit ironic, considering that you've spent most of your career falling on your arse!')

\* \* \*

Peter Eade, a young theatrical agent who had recently started his own business, was a regular attender at the RADA end-of-term productions and had had his eye on me for some time. After seeing me as the mother in Noël Coward's *Peace in Our Time* he wrote me a letter, suggesting that I visit him in his office for a chat.

Ever the innocent, I reacted to this idea with horror. Visit an agent in his office? *In his office?* All that stuff about casting couches, and about how impressionable young actresses got parts through the exercise of talents other than thespian, was the staple matter of our coffee-bar gossip, and I wasn't going to get involved in that sort of thing, thank you very much. I threw the letter away.

A little while later my friend Bill Becker, another RADA student, asked whether I had heard from a man called Peter Eade, and I confessed that although I had indeed received a letter, I had not followed it up. I explained my misgivings, upon which Bill convinced me that they were, in Peter's case at least, completely misplaced; he added that Peter was going to be one of the top agents, and I'd be mad to ignore a letter from him. He even offered to come along with me and hold my hand. I took him up on this offer, and a few days later Bill and I made our way to Peter's Cork Street office for my first meeting with the man who was to be my agent and friend for the next thirty years.

The moment I walked in I realised how ludicrous my worries had been. Peter was young (scarcely much older than myself) and completely charming, and immediately inspired trust and confidence. Having set up his own agency, he was trying to build up a select list of actors to represent, adamant that he would keep his operation on a small scale so that he could give each client a proper amount of care and attention. At that time he had only a handful of performers on his books, but they included Ronnie Barker, with whom I would work on television in years to come, and Rosalind Knight (daughter of the very distinguished actor Esmond Knight), who would appear with me in *Carry On Nurse* (as Nurse Nightingale) and *Carry On Teacher* (in which she – as Felicity Wheeler – and I have a drunken brawl in the staff room). I was one of Peter's very early signings; within a year I had been joined in his stable by Rachel Roberts and a rather individual young actor by the name of Kenneth Williams.

It is impossible to exaggerate the importance for an aspiring actor of your first agent, and in Peter Eade I had found the ideal guide and mentor: never one to be concerned just with the ten per cent, soon he was not just looking after the business side of my career but also a valued friend and adviser, and I found myself sharing my concerns, personal as well as professional, with him much more often than with my parents.

But, great agent as he was, even Peter could not propel me straight into starring roles in the West End, and the first two years after leaving RADA were spent cutting my teeth in that most demanding of theatrical environments – rep.

Repertory theatre – far more popular in those days than it seems to be now – involved a company based in one place putting on a varied diet of plays, with the programme changing regularly, and for an actor this meant a demanding schedule of learning one role while simultaneously performing another. It also meant staying in strange digs in all sorts of exotic locations around the country – for me none more exotic than the Lancashire town where I had my first taste of rep: Chorlton-cum-Hardy, where I spent nine dismal weeks in the autumn of 1950.

Leaving home, never previously having spent more than a few days away from Station House, was a terrific wrench, for my parents as much as for me. My departure was a traumatic moment for them and they did not try to hide their concern, but they accepted my going as part and parcel of the agreement we'd made that they would do all they could to support my theatrical career, and after a great deal of my mother fussing around and my father trying to keep her calm, a few tears were shed on both sides, and I was off on the train. Chorlton here I cum!

What went on in the theatre is only a part of what made acting in rep such a deeply educational experience, for the real star turn in any actor's memory of rep is . . . the landlady.

All actors who have come through the rep experience have a fund of stories of the female grotesques who have ruled over their digs while they were on the road. (A favourite of mine concerns the young actor who brings home some fresh asparagus for his supper and leaves it on the kitchen table while he goes upstairs to change. On his return downstairs his landlady tells him, 'I've put your violets in a vase.')

The *grande dame* of my digs at Chorlton-cum-Hardy was Mrs Phelan, a somewhat overweight lady whose principal interest in life at that time was perspiring, most profusely when presiding over the large Aga which formed the centrepiece of her kitchen.

'Ooh, I've got one of me sweats coming on,' she'd tell me forebodingly as she took the towel from the Aga rail and wiped her teeming forehead with it – then proceeded to use that same towel to take out our evening meal, a move guaranteed to make my appetite promptly disappear.

Mrs Phelan's establishment was not a great place for fixtures and fittings. In my bedroom the curtains and carpet were threadbare and the only light was a bare bulb overhead, so bright that I had to buy a bag of fruit from the local shop and use the brown bag it came in to act as a sort of impromptu lampshade. Despite this stratagem, the light given off by the bulb was so dazzling that I found it impossible to learn lines (never one of my favourite occupations) up in my room. Mrs Phelan, though, clearly thought I was making too much use of the facility, as her usual good-night to me was 'Don't leave that floody light on all night!' A woman of high principle, she refused to use to let the word 'bloody' pass her lips and resorted to 'floody' in all sorts of circumstances ('It's a floody tip in here!'). One night I came in late after a party and there at the top of the stairs was this malevolent presence: Mrs Phelan in her night attire, complete with curlers and hairnet.

'What floody time of night do you call this? Get to floody bed!'

Another inhabitant of Mrs Phelan's household was her mother, who was as artful as a wagonload of monkeys. She had a way of seducing me into doing the ironing for her when Mrs Phelan herself was out, insisting that her aches and pains meant she couldn't manage it herself. (I was to exact my revenge on Mrs Phelan's mother much later in my career by using her as a model for characters like Gran in *Till Death Us Do Part*.)

Still, for all the aggravations and the sweat, the food (despite that towel) was very wholesome and my bed was clean.

Rep was a real baptism of fire into the acting profession. At drama school you had a whole term to learn and rehearse a part before exposing yourself to the public; in rep you're learning and rehearsing one role during the day and performing another in the evening, every day of the week except Sundays. It was very intense work. To make it worse, this was my first time away from home and I felt extremely lonely during those dark, cold days up in Chorlton-cum-Hardy – so lonely and homesick that at times I seriously thought of giving the whole thing up. Suddenly that typing pool in the insurance office in London did not seem quite so unappealing: at least it would have been warm and well lit, and there might have been a few friendly faces around . . .

The rep routine went something like this. Wake up in the morning at about eight, swallow a quick breakfast, go off to the theatre, spend the morning rehearsing the following week's play, short break for lunch, then continue rehearsing, knock off at about four or five, back to the digs for a quick meal, back to the theatre, into costume and make-up, do the performance, finish about half past ten, out of costume, take off make-up, back into civvy clothes, get back to digs and start learning more lines from the play you were rehearsing that week. The rest of the day was your own.

In theory you had Sunday off, but the great majority of actors I knew in rep were so anxious at the thought of opening on the Monday in the play they'd started rehearsing only the previous Monday that they'd spend all day Sunday swotting up their part; for me, straight from RADA and its comparatively leisurely schedules, this anxiety was compounded by the dreadful shock to the system of the weekly treadmill.

After a month in small roles with the Chorlton-cum-Hardy players I was selected for my first leading part: the title role in a play called *Sarah Simple*. My initial reaction was one of horror, and most of me wanted to run away, but I knew that if I were serious about my acting career I had to knuckle down and get on with it: *Sarah Simple* at Chorlton-cum-Hardy was scarcely the National Theatre, but it was a step in the right direction. (In rep, by the way, playing the lead did not mean a quick route to riches: you got paid the same, whatever the size of your part.)

The cast of *Sarah Simple* included a young actor who would make it very big and whom I was to encounter again in *Carry On Screaming!* as well as in television comedy. Like me, Harry H. Corbett was starting at the bottom but fired with dreams of the top. I didn't get to know him very well at Chorlton-cum-Hardy rep, not least because all the boys had one dressing room and all the girls another, and there was not the free-and-easy atmosphere which pervaded some theatrical companies.

My terror at the exposure awaiting me as leading lady in *Sarah Simple* was multiplied on the Monday when I started to take a proper look at the script. I can still see the bloody – floody – thing in my mind's eye: a bright blue cover, and line upon line upon line of speech for the title role. I can't now remember the plot, but I can vividly recall how that script looked after I'd taken a pen to it and underlined my bits: it was awash with red ink.

Floody light or no floody light, I had to get down to learning those lines as fast as I could, as Friday was the day when we had to put our books down and rehearse with our lines properly committed to memory. On that Monday I rushed back to my digs as soon the curtain came down on the evening performance and started to go over the lines. On the Tuesday I rushed back quicker, and sat up late into the night madly trying to cram them in. Wednesday and Thursday saw that floody light burned to exploding point, but the harder I tried, the more I panicked.

I arrived at the theatre on the fateful Friday a blubbering wreck. I got precious little sympathy from the other four girls in the company. My first couple of roles at Chorlton had attracted some nice notices in the local press, and that old green-eyed monster was rearing its ugly head, to the extent that the other girls were becoming quite off-hand with me: saying hello in the morning was about as much conversation as they were prepared to indulge in before they returned to talking among themselves, leaving me feeling very excluded.

They'd taken against me even more now I'd got the main part in *Sarah Simple* – someone had to play it, for heaven's sake! – and were giving me the cold shoulder. It all made for a very sour atmosphere.

One of the male actors was more supportive. Seeing that I had worked myself up into a real state, he took me along to see Mrs Spreckley, wife of Arthur Spreckley, who ran the company. She calmed me down, assured me that she could persuade her husband to let me use the book for that day's rehearsal (which she did), and suggested that I go round to their house on the Sunday – the day before the play opened – to get word perfect.

I turned up on Sunday morning, was put into the right frame of mind with a wonderful roast lunch, and then got down to work. Mrs Spreckley took me though the whole play, scene by scene, and somehow managed to instil the confidence that I could do the role. Her last words to me as I left the house that Sunday evening were: 'I guarantee that you'll go on that stage tomorrow and be word perfect.' I did – and I was.

Five weeks after that I put the fleshpots of Chorlton-cum-Hardy behind me. It took a little white lie to get me released – I told them my mother was ill and needed me back home – but I knew that I had to get back to Station House for some home comforts, and so that's where I headed. It hardly needs saying that my mother and father were delighted to have me back while I waited to see what might turn up next.

Not long before Christmas 1950 I had a message to call Miss Pilgrim, the secretary at RADA. My first thought was 'Oh, God – they've found me out and want my certificate back,' but in fact she had welcome news. Chorus girls were needed for a pantomime in Salisbury. Two other girls from RADA were going. Was I interested?

Of course I was – and within a couple of days the three of us were shivering our way down to Salisbury on the train. As we arrived it was just beginning to snow, but we made our way from the station to the theatre to collect the list of local digs in (to coin a phrase) high spirits. Two hours later those spirits had slipped considerably. The snow had started falling heavily and was already settling, and the sight of these three forlorn figures trudging from house to house looking for digs, knocking forlornly on doors and always being turned away, must have been like something out of *A Christmas Carol*. It was getting dark, and we were just beginning to think that we would never get warm again, and would probably have to lie down huddled together in a snowdrift and await the inevitable death.

By teatime we were freezing cold and aching with hunger, and as night was rapidly coming on it was with a rising sense of despair that we knocked on the door of yet another house on our rapidly diminishing list. The door was swiftly opened – and there was a scene straight off a Victorian Christmas card: merry, welcoming faces, roaring log fire, crumpets toasting, the lot! We three frozen waifs were ushered in and seated in front of the fire, toasted crumpet put into one hand, cup of tea into the other – and within a few minutes were beginning to feel human again. Our saviours turned out to be David Doddimead and James Cairncross, fellow actors at the Salisbury Arts Company – who were putting on the pantomime – and we spent a magical couple of hours warming ourselves through and swapping theatrical gossip. Their place was too small to accommodate three girls, but they pointed us in the right direction – towards a small and very modest hotel where we were finally taken in. Here the three of us snuggled together in three single beds in the one room, where we soon learned to keep body and soul together on bread toasted in front of the one-bar electric fire, washed down with glasses of milk. The room cost us £2 10s each per week, exactly half of the £5 a week we were earning for our two shows every day.

Although I had been cast simply as a chorus girl, my singing ability stood me in good stead when I was picked out to assist the comic during the audience singalong interlude, and my performance must have gone down well with Peter Potter, who directed the more highbrow productions at Salisbury, because at the end of the panto run he suggested that I stay on. One of the company's resident actresses might be about to emigrate to Australia, which would leave a vacancy. The snag was that if she didn't go there'd be no opening. I decided to take the risk and remained with the company in Salisbury for a short while, but in the event the opening never materialised, and I had to be on my way – with Peter's promise that he'd use me again as soon as the opportunity arose.

I continued to make my way in rep during 1951, and was in Luton on 9 May for my twenty-first birthday. Roy Nightingale, a friend of Peter Eade's and an actor with the Luton company, bought me a bottle of champagne – the first but, happily, not the last of my life – and the rest of the cast presented me with a cake and a card in the shape of a silver key.

It's impossible to know just how you build up acting experience, but it was during one production at Luton that I gave myself some evidence that I was, at the very least, learning how to think on my feet. The play was called *On Monday Next* and concerned, appropriately enough, a company of rep actors. With business such as the writer having to scribble the script on toilet rolls as he couldn't find enough paper, the piece was something of an in-joke and of potentially more interest and enjoyment to the actors than the audience – what the acting fraternity calls 'proey'.

I played Daphne, the *ingénue*, and for most of the time I was on stage had to carry round a little poodle.

One matinée we were really up against it. The audience was very sparse and was mostly made up of old ladies in hats, who were more interested in polishing off the cups of tea they had been served during the interval than in what was taking place on stage: we weren't getting any laughs at all – which when you're playing what you think is a comedy is a deeply lowering experience. Maybe it was just that the play was *too* 'proey' – but there was nothing we could do to get the audience to respond.

Every line was dying a death, and although this left the audience stony-faced, to us up on stage it was desperately funny – so funny that during one of my scenes with my poodle I started to get a fit of the giggles. I tried like mad to suppress them, but my efforts proved useless once I noticed a rivulet of gleaming liquid had started making its way steadily down the stage, stopping only as it reached the footlights. By now the entire company was in fits of laughter, and all I could do was tap the little poodle on his backside:

'You naughty boy – look what you've done!'

But I don't think the old ladies in hats laughed even then.

Towards the end of the year Peter Eade got a call from Peter Potter offering me the role of principal girl in *The Happy Ha'penny*, a new pantomime at the Glasgow Citizens' Theatre, so I packed my bags and made my way to the frozen north. The Citizens' Theatre is situated in the Gorbals, which in those days was a decidedly seedy area, and had been doing great work in bringing theatre to a community not overburdened with opportunities for culture. (The first panto that Myles Rudge wrote was for the Citizens' Theatre, and understandably he felt very apprehensive about how it would go down with the Glasgow audience – the more so when he learned that one of the dress rehearsals was to be a freebie for local children from the Gorbals, not likely to be the most receptive audience for Myles's urbane wit. After that dress rehearsal he was leaving the theatre when he saw one ten-year-old Glaswegian urchin turn to another and ask what he'd thought of the performance. 'Oh,' said the kid, 'it was fockin' maaaagic!')

*The Happy Ha'penny* had one of the most joyous companies I ever had the good fortune to work with. Stanley Baxter was the Dame, Joan Seton principal boy, Madeleine Christie the fairy queen – and Jimmy Gilbert, later Head of Light Entertainment at the BBC, was in the chorus.

If Luton had taught me one valuable lesson which would stand me in good stead throughout my acting career – blame the nearest available dog – I learned another, far more fundamental, in Glasgow.

On Fridays, after we had been paid, a group of us – normally myself, Ian McNaughton, Joan Seton and Jimmy Copeland – would go for lunch together, and one particular Friday we found ourselves in a typically noisy and bustling Glasgow pub, where I was handed a half-pint of beer. I'd never drunk beer before and didn't much take to it. Then we went off for lunch, and the glass of wine I had with my meal did not mix well with the beer. After lunch we went to the cinema to see *Cyrano de Bergerac* with José Ferrer, and I could hardly keep my eyes open during the film. As we came out of the cinema we bumped into a Scottish friend of Ian's.

After a great deal of 'Howyadoin, then?' he demanded that we all go and have a wee dram before the show, which was all very well for seasoned drinkers like the men but a riskier proposition for a true *ingénue* like me. After we'd settled into our seats in the nearest bar (this being Glasgow in the 1950s, there were parts of the pub from which ladies were excluded), they offered me a drink. I was feeling a little woozy from lunchtime so declined anything alcoholic, but the Scottish friend would not hear of such timidity: 'Och, I'll get ye something that'll put ye on your feet' – and before I knew it three Martinis were whizzing around my bloodstream.

Back at the theatre, I somehow managed to get my make-up on and get through my first entrance, but I knew that trouble lay ahead. Although my role in *The Happy Ha'penny* was, unusually for pantomime principal girls, a fairly robust comic part, at one point I had to sing a Hebridean love song. Resplendent in medieval costume, topped with a high-coned hat from which a piece of tulle wafted, I had to stand on the side of the stage, close to the wings, trilling:

> Thou hast left me ever, Jamie!
> Thou hast left me ever . . .

That Friday evening I performed the song closer to the wings than usual: I was so overcome with drink that Jimmy Copeland had to stand behind the curtain at the side of the stage, with a vice-like grip on my elbow to keep me upright. I was more worried about falling into the footlights than about Jamie having left me ever. Blow Jamie: it was Jimmy who was much more important at that moment, and somehow I managed to get through the number without disaster.

I came offstage dripping with sweat, and I swore that I'd never again have a drink before a performance. I never did.

## 3

# 'Any Dead Wood in That Show of Yours, Joan?'

My career was soon gathering momentum, and before long I was getting involved in the brave new world of television. Although very much in its infancy in the early 1950s (the BBC was the only channel until ITV started in 1955), it was clearly the coming medium – and for an aspiring actress it represented untold glamour and fame.

Just my luck, then, that my first television role should require that I be heard but not seen, providing some of the voices for the children's puppet show *Vegetable Village*. It may have been a modest beginning in television, but at least I was able to demonstrate my acting versatility, as I had to play three characters: Millicent Mushroom, Barbara Beetroot and – to underline that I had not lost that RADA skill in interpreting a male role – Oscar Onion.

The dialogue was mostly along the lines of:

– Hallo! I'm Oscar Onion, and I'm going out to play today. I wonder if Barbara Beetroot would like to join me. Are you coming out today, Barbara Beetroot?

– No, I don't think so, Oscar Onion . . .

It wasn't much, but it was a start.

Meanwhile, I was now getting more and more involved in revue, and life became very hectic. At one point I was working as assistant stage manager for the Grand Guignol plays at the Irving Theatre Club, situated above an Indian restaurant near Leicester Square, then rushing off to perform in a revue called *The Bells of St Martin's* – which is where I first met Hattie Jacques – then tearing back to the Irving to take part in another revue, *Just Lately*. I also understudied Gabrielle Broom and Betty Marsden in another late-night revue, *Ten Fifteen*, which added to my rapidly increasing experience.

The essence of 'intimate revue' was variety, which was the core of its great appeal for me: it was frothy and bubbly, and tearing around backstage, getting out of one costume and pulling myself into another in time for the next turn, gave every evening an air of great excitement. A small group of actors would perform a quick-fire succession of items – songs, comic sketches, short plays – often with a satirical core which was always liable to be updated just before a performance to give the piece a topical edge, and its intimacy was based on a close rapport with the audience, which made it ideal for small theatres and theatre clubs.

Theatres didn't come much smaller than the Irving, which was about the size of a matchbox – and proprietors didn't come much larger than its owner Mr Chaudhuri (who also owned the restaurant downstairs). His theatre club did not go in for niceties like separate dressing facilities for the men and the women, so all the actors in *Just Lately* changed together in one small space under the stage, with us – Jasmine Dee, Rosaline Haddon, Viv Pickles and myself – separated from them – Kenneth Connor, Dennis Egan and Charles Ross – by a line of mirrors which were placed on the large table in the middle of the room.

At least these excessively spartan conditions made for a wonderful team spirit, and that feeling extended to the writers, with whom I would continue to work in revue for years: David Climie, who wrote most of the sketches, and John Pritchett and Ronnie Cass, who were responsible for the music. Our director was my old mate from RADA Ronnie Stevens.

My big moment in *Just Lately* was 'Diary of a Queen', in which I got myself up as the holiday beauty queen Miss Potting Hill in bathing costume, red sash, fishnet tights and tottering high heels – the whole effect topped with a crown – and sang about my life as a holiday beauty queen:

> . . . And I got a kiss from Maxwell Reid
> That's how I bruised my knee
> Oh, the life of a holiday queen is ever so gay!

I never understood what that meant (and still don't), but as it always got a huge laugh, who was I to complain?

Revue was providing me with wonderful experience, but more than anything I hankered to get into films, and during the run of *Just Lately* at the Irving I had a call from Peter Eade: he had arranged for me to go down to the Associated British Pictures studio to meet the casting director, John Redway.

My old terror of auditions came back to haunt me as I made my way down to Elstree, but John Redway was charming, and after introducing himself got straight down to business.

'Would you mind walking up and down the room?'

Oh, God! I thought, Here we go! – but I knew that I was never going to get anywhere as an actress unless I forced myself through the ordeal of auditioning, and I started to walk up the room in my best Rank Charm School manner.

I walked up the room. I walked down the room. I sat down. I got up. I answered all his questions in my best twittering Minnie Ann voice. But afterwards on my way back to London I knew that however gracefully I had performed – Mabel Temperley would have thought her ten pounds well invested – I had not impressed John Redway enough. I was well aware that I was capable of doing better than that, but I was resigned to rejection.

A couple of days later Peter rang with the

inevitable verdict. John had liked me, but had thought that there wasn't a great deal of – how should he put it? – *passion* in how I performed. Although John would bear me in mind for possible roles, Peter stressed that I should not hold out too much hope: 'He's not sure you're right for films.'

A couple of weeks later Peter called again. Amazing news: John Redway had come to see *Just Lately* the night before and couldn't believe that the Joan Sims milking every laugh off the audience with her Miss Potting Hill was the same Joan Sims who had produced that passionless walk up and down his office. He had changed his mind about my potential for the silver screen, and would be putting me up for a film part.

So it was that I found myself on the set of *Will Any Gentleman?*, a comedy directed by Michael Anderson (who later directed *The Dam Busters* and *Around the World in Eighty Days*) and starring George Cole as a meek and mild little fellow whose character is transformed by a hypnotist. The supporting cast included two actors who would go on to play Doctor Who, William Hartnell and Jon Pertwee (with whom I'd later work in *Worzel Gummidge*), as well as Sid James (our first time working together) and Lionel Jeffries.

To be strictly accurate, *Will Any Gentleman?*, released in 1953, was not my first feature film, as I played a small role in *Colonel March Investigates*, a B-movie released in 1952 and cobbled together from episodes of a television series which – with all due respect to Millicent Mushroom and Oscar Onion – had supplied my first 'real' small screen role.

Colonel March himself, head of Department D3 at Scotland Yard (otherwise known as the Department of Queer Complaints), was played by none other than Boris Karloff, long a household name as a consequence of all those appearances as Frankenstein's monster and other assorted ghouls. To me he was a hero – one of those Hollywood greats I had drooled over (or, in his case, shrunk from) at the Radion Cinema back in Laindon – and the chance to appear with him so early in my own career set me all of a flutter: I was very nervous before the filming and went over my lines again and again and again. Not that I had that many lines to learn. I was playing Marjorie Dawson, Colonel March's secretary, and my few moments on screen were mostly spent taking calls from clients anxious to have the intrepid Colonel March set about solving the latest supernatural mystery haunting London.

My nerves were not helped by the fear that the real Boris Karloff might be like the on-screen Boris Karloff and start doing unspeakable things to me, but he turned out to be very docile and sweet, more inclined to talk about gardening than wander round the countryside terrorising the natives.

By now I had found myself doing so much work in or around London that I had decided the time had come for me to move up from Essex. My first London home (if that's not too strong a word) was a tiny room in a house in Earls Court. It was seedy and dirty, the loo was three flights of stairs away, and the bathroom another two flights beyond that; none of the sinks in the house had ever had so much as a whiff of Vim. In comparison, the sweaty Mrs Phelan's establishment in Chorlton-cum-Hardy was a palace. But it was my own bolthole, and it gave me a wonderful and novel feeling of independence.

Once I'd settled in I wrote home: when are you coming up to see me? The following week my mother duly arrived to cast her beady eye over the conditions in which her Joan was living in the wicked city, and – no great surprise – she did not share my romantic view of domestic bliss. The more she looked round the room, the more horrified she became. 'Your father would die if he saw you living in conditions like this,' she declared, and I knew that the clock was ticking over my stay in Earls Court.

Sure enough, she saw to it that I was out within a couple of days, removed to the much more salubrious surroundings of Hamilton Place in the refined north London district of St John's Wood, where I had heard that a room was available in the house of the actor Ronald Adam. This was more to my mother's liking: Ronald and his wife had a son and a daughter, and there was a very strong family atmosphere around the house. Indeed, it was an atmosphere that I soon found myself envying: there had never been that feeling of togetherness at Station House, and the sense of both unity and liberation about the Adam household made me realise what I'd been missing.

My fee for my part in *Will Any Gentleman?* was £25. To me this felt like a fortune, and as soon as I received the money I went straight out and opened a building society account . . . Actually, no. I took myself promptly to the West End and blew the lot to indulge my growing obsession with – wait for it – kitchen equipment: the best in the way of cutlery, crockery and culinary machinery that Selfridges could provide. Where this craving for acquiring domestic goods came from I've no idea, but it presented an immediate practical problem, as my room in St John's Wood was scarcely large enough to house my booty. Ronald Adam, highly amused by his young lodger's blowing her earnings in such an eccentric way, went out and found two stout orange boxes to serve as a makeshift cupboard.

Dipping my toe into the worlds of film and television was all very exciting, but the bread and butter continued to come from the stage, and the same writing team who had worked on *Just Lately* asked me to join a revue at the New Lindsey Theatre Club in Notting Hill. This was *Intimacy at Eight*, whose cast included Leslie Crowther, Eunice Gayson, Dilys Laye, Peter Felgate and a young actor whom Ronnie Cass and his co-writer Peter Myers had spotted in the end-of-term show at the London School of Economics: Ron Moody had so impressed them at the LSE on the Friday evening that by Monday morning he had been recruited to our company.

'Intimacy' was about the right word for conditions backstage at the New Lindsey. During a freezing winter all the actors – boys and girls alike – shared one dressing room, and there was no running water: the ASM would come in and plonk a bowl of water in the middle of the room, and that had to supply all our needs.

After its stint at the New Lindsey, the revue was revamped – lots of new material added, lots of old material ditched – and under the name *High Spirits* set off on a five-week tour prior to opening in the West End.

Our travels took us as far north as Aberdeen, where the showbiz page of the local paper carried a photograph of a voluptuous young actress: 'Coldest girl in chilly Aberdeen last week was, surely, scantily-clad Joan Simms, singing the lament of an artist's model in the "High Spirits" revue.' All publicity was good publicity, I suppose, even if they couldn't spell my name right.

It was on this tour of the frozen wastes that Ian Carmichael (who had been brought in for *High Spirits*, though he had not been in *Intimacy at Eight*), Dilys Laye, John Walters (our ASM) and I took digs with the famous Mr and Mrs Dunbar. I say Mr and Mrs Dunbar, but in all honesty we never actually set eyes on Mrs. We imagined her cooking madly away down in her subterranean kitchen, like something out of *Sweeney Todd*, preparing all those wonderful meals which were brought up to the dining room by her husband.

As soon as he had served us our food, Mr

Dunbar would start doing what he did best in life: hover.

'Is everything all right with your meal?'

'Yes, thank you, Mr Dunbar.'

He carried on hovering.

'Are you enjoying your supper?'

'Yes, thank you, Mr Dunbar.'

Once we'd started to see the funny side of Mr Dunbar's desperation to please, our attempts to stop him hovering and leave us in peace to eat our supper became a little comic routine in itself.

He'd lean over the table and stare into our chomping faces to see if we were really enjoying our meal.

'Can I fetch you anything else?'

'No, thank you ever so much, Mr Dunbar. Please don't feel you have to wait, Mr Dunbar.'

Quiet for another minute, then:

'Is everything all right?'

'Yes, thank you, Mr Dunbar. We'll let you know when we're ready for our next course.'

Dear Mr Dunbar: how could we tell him his presence was giving us indigestion?

In May 1953 *High Spirits* opened in the West End at the London Hippodrome in Leicester Square – a large theatre, possibly too large to be a comfortable home for intimate revue. (One morning during the run our director Billie Chappell was greeted by a friend as he hurried across Leicester Square. 'Can't stop now,' shouted Billie, 'I'm just going to shrink the Hippodrome!')

After the first performance we all repaired to a nearby watering hole for an impromptu party, while one of the company went down to Fleet Street to pick up the first editions of the morning papers. As soon as he came back we fell upon the review pages – whatever our fate, we had to know it as soon as possible – and the first one I grabbed was the *Daily Telegraph*. I frantically searched for the review pages, and there, under the byline of W. A. Darlington, it was:

There is a real and very welcome touch of originality about 'High Spirits' at the Hippodrome. It is an intimate revue, on a big scale. It has the intelligence and the style which is usually associated with neat little shows in small theatres and it does not rely on a big company or spectacular scenes.

Yet it has the necessary size and sweep to fill the big Hippodrome and to rouse last night's responsive audience to a notable pitch of enthusiasm. The show is indeed a most judicious mixture of cleverness and popular appeal.

Yes yes yes, but what about the actors? Mr Darlington went on to praise the main performers, and then, in the very last paragraph of his review, came the mention I'd been looking for:

The average of talent is high. Ian Carmichael is outstanding, and Joan Sims and Valerie Carton distinguished themselves . . .

Recognition at last!

The first half of *High Spirits* – a very lavish production, with décor and period costumes designed by the artist and cartoonist Osbert Lancaster – consisted of a brisk run through the previous four centuries of British history, depicted in different songs and sketches – such as a 1708 version of the radio soap opera *Mrs Dale's Diary*, or 'A Smile, a Song and a Lexicon', a cross-talk act about Johnson's *Dictionary* between Cyril Ritchard and Ian Carmichael.

My solo turn in this helter-skelter history lesson was a point number – verse spoken to music – set in 1868: 'Inveterate Poseur', the piece which had evoked the sympathy of the local paper in Aberdeen. All got up to make a suitably Greek impression in pale green chiffon, I was the artist's model desperate for a respite from posing ('Ooh, Lord Leighton – may I rest now?') before launching into her lament:

Ever since Lord Elgin found those nasty marbles
Every painting must be classic, if you please;
So I pose as Aphrodite
In this skimpy little nightie
And I understand what's meant by Grecian freeze.

The first half of the show ended with 'The Shopgirl Princess' (described as 'A Modern Musical Comedy'), set in a department store called Garrods, complete with that wonderful system of wires by which cash was whizzed around.

After the break – the programme specified an

'interval of thirty-five years' – the show concentrated on the present day, and anyone who thinks that the post-war satire boom began with *Beyond the Fringe* in 1961 should consider some of the material which those 1950s revues were putting out. The second half of *High Spirits* contained several acts with a real edge, pieces which put across politically loaded material under the disguise of amiable revue sketches. There was, for example, a piece by David Climie and Ronald Cass called 'The Plea', a very ironic and pointed look at life under apartheid in South Africa. This song, with its refrain of 'Don't malign Malan' (Dr Daniel Malan was Prime Minister of South Africa), was performed by Marie Bryant, a black singer from New York, and it caused an outcry. The authorities in South Africa kicked up a fuss, a leader in the *New York Times* denounced the notion of bringing over an American black girl to sing such a song, and Dr Malan himself made it known that he was so offended he would not be coming to the Coronation, though eventually he changed his mind. (One evening Ronnie Cass went into Marie Bryant's dressing room to find her standing in the middle of the floor, stark naked. 'Honey,' she exclaimed, 'if I'd known you were coming I'd have shaved!')

The show also contained some pretty highbrow pieces which I had considerable difficulty understanding, though I was too shy to own up to this – that Elgin Marbles song, for example, or 'A La Sartre', an excerpt from a musical based on existential philosophy, whatever that may have been! Valerie Carton felt as much in the dark as I was, and the poor dear spent the first week of the run at the local library trying to work out what some of the jokes were about . . .

If some of *High Spirits* went over the head of members of the cast, what hope had the audiences got? It was all very well to take the attitude expressed by some of the writing team, that 'If the audience don't know what we're on about, then they bloody well should do,' but that didn't put bums on seats, and the show closed at the Hippodrome after about three months – but not before my mother had proudly made the trip from Laindon to see her daughter in action: the only time, I think, that either of my parents saw me perform professionally.

Regular appearances in revue were not making it easy for me to create a name for myself as a straight actress; an added problem was the disadvantage of having, as the director Anthony Asquith put it at one audition, 'far too happy a face'. Although I did not want to find myself typecast so early in my career, I was getting more and more offers to play comic roles. The parts themselves ranged from small to minute, but I was soon working with some of the top screen comics of the day.

*Meet Mr Lucifer*, directed by Arnold Ridley (who later found a permanent place in the nation's affections as Private Godfrey in *Dad's Army*), introduced me to the legendary Ealing Studios. Based around the familiar world of a flea-bitten pantomime production, the film was a satire on the acting profession at a time when television was threatening the popularity of the theatre, and starred Stanley Holloway, with my old friend Ian Carmichael playing Man Friday. I had a tiny part as the fairy queen – and pretty much all I can remember about it now is that it was the first time I was ever flown across the stage on a kirby wire!

To be acting with a star as big as Stanley Holloway sounds very grand, but in truth my part was so tiny that I was only filming for a day or two and had very little to do with the big names. The same applied to my first film with Norman Wisdom, *Trouble in Store*. Norman was one of the biggest stars of the day, but my part was so small that I hardly encountered him. I also landed a part in a film about boxing, *The Square Ring*.

Those three films were all released in 1953, and the same year brought to the screen the first of the *Doctor* films which enjoyed such lasting popularity.

Filmed at Pinewood Studios in Buckinghamshire, *Doctor in the House* was produced by Betty Box, one of the first really powerful women in the film industry, whose knack of giving the cinemagoing public exactly what they wanted earned her the nickname 'Betty Box Office'. She was married to Peter Rogers (soon to enter this story as producer of the *Carry On* films), and her director on *Doctor in the House* was Ralph Thomas, elder brother of *Carry On* director Gerald.

Playing a character who gloried in the name of Nurse Rigor Mortis, I had just one scene in *Doctor in the House*, but since that scene was with the dreamboat to end all dreamboats, Dirk Bogarde playing the handsome Dr Simon Sparrow, my pre-filming nerves were even more taut than usual – which Dirk promptly sensed, and just before we started filming he presented me with a large box of Black Magic chocolates. This charming gesture increased rather than calmed my palpitations, but I managed to control myself sufficiently to play the scene.

Having been persuaded by his fellow student doctors to make a play for Nurse Mortis, Simon Sparrow tries to cosy up to her on the sofa as she sits there obstructing his attempts to kiss her by noisily munching an apple. He turns out the light, but any hopes of a seduction scene begin to fade as soon as Nurse Mortis opens her mouth and, in her high-pitched, lisping voice, tells him:

–I had an awful job to get here tonight. I had to swap my late duty with Nurse Gibson's bedpans.
–Ohh . . .
–That was just before we had that awful case where we had to use the stomach pump.
–Look: would you rather have some cocoa? . . .

*Doctor in the House* was a huge success, and my tiny role as the frigid Nurse Mortis proved a great boost to my career. Peter Rogers had noticed me in the film and – no doubt encouraged by his wife –

offered me a part in *To Dorothy a Son*, starring Shelley Winters and John Gregson, then right at the pinnacle of his popularity: *Genevieve*, in which he featured with Kenneth More (who had himself starred alongside Dirk Bogarde in *Doctor in the House*), was released the same year.

Most of my early film parts were in comic roles, but *The Sea Shall Not Have Them*, starring Dirk Bogarde and Michael Redgrave, was a much more serious affair, the story of the survivors of a seaplane crash awaiting rescue in a dinghy. It did have its comic moments for me, however.

I was playing a wife whose husband has gone missing at sea, and one of my scenes involved my anxiously asking Griffith Jones whether there was any news. The scene was shot on location at a railway station, where unfortunately we were positioned just outside the gents. There must have been some malfunctioning of the sluices that day, as each time I asked desperately about what had become of my husband, Griffith Jones's reply was accompanied by a great hissing and whooshing noise from the other side of the wall behind us – followed by the cry of 'Cut!' from our increasingly exasperated director.

Griffith was a great giggler, and the more our highly dramatic scene was interrupted by the plumbing, the more he'd collapse with laughter. With each successive take I tried a new way to avoid catching his eye. I'd stare at the buttons on his jacket, gaze at the braid on his cap, or try to look way beyond him; but the entire unit soon latched on, which made matters even worse. Eventually we had to move to a quieter part of the station and stage the whole scene again.

*The Belles of St Trinian's*, made at Shepperton Studios and released in 1954, has long been established as one of the best-loved British comedy films of all time, principally on account of Alastair Sim's dual roles as the headmistress Miss Fritton and her bookmaker brother Clarence. St Trinian's was staffed by a glorious collection of bizarre teachers (half of them on the run from the law) including Beryl Reid, Renée Houston and Irene Handl, and I had a cameo role as the seductive biology mistress Miss Dawn – first discovered in the staff room fixing a pin-up of her favourite boxer to the cupboard door – which gave me another chance to wear the sort of flowing Veronica Lake-style blonde wig I sported for 'Siren Song' later that year.

I was becoming more and more matey with the dancer Eleanor Fazan, universally known as 'Fiz'. Having worked together in several revues, we were soon close friends, and when she asked me whether I wanted to join her in a luxury flat on the Bayswater Road overlooking Hyde Park – rent free – I jumped at the chance to move out of my digs in St John's Wood and move to where the fun was.

Fiz's godfather was Sir Charles Vyner-Brooke, the last white Rajah of Sarawak, and he had bought the flat for his wife the Rani to use on her visits to London. Fortunately such visits were very few and far between, and he offered the use of the flat to Fiz – who then invited me to join her.

My mother was enormously impressed by Fiz's aristocratic connections, and our frequent visits down to Laindon helped convince my parents that I was not ruining myself up in the wicked city: if I had a friend and flat-mate as nice and reliable as Fiz, I must be keeping myself in the right company. And my father – who was immensely proud of my acting achievements, and subjected visitors to a detailed perusal of his scrapbooks of my career – used to love it when I took Fiz down. He'd try to impress by adopting what he rather quaintly thought was the 'in' language of the London theatre, asking me: 'Any dead wood in that show of yours, Joan?'

Back in London, each day was hectic – tearing around from theatre to film studio to audition to dance class and then back to the theatre – and our social life could be as frenetic as the work. Our regular haunt after finishing at the theatre each evening was Harry Green's night club in Soho, where we would dance for hours or sit at the small tables on the edge of the dance floor and eat bacon and eggs washed down with green chartreuse. There was a spotlight which roamed around the room picking out people at the different tables; more and more often that spotlight was picking out Fiz cosying up to the composer Stanley Myers. Before long they were inseparable, and eventually married. (Stanley sadly died in 1993.)

Having found such happiness, Fiz – influenced too, no doubt, by the smooth sounds of the Nat

King Cole records which we played incessantly in the flat – was determined that I should get some romance into my own life, and since I was not seeing anyone at the time, she decided to act on my behalf.

The result was The Blind Date From Hell.

Fiz discovered that her friend Twizzie – a merciful abbreviation of something like Elizabeth Twittington-Hoggins – had a brother who was a medical student in London and who, according to Twizzie, needed to get out more. Fiz had never met this brother, but rapidly put two and two together and decided that he would be the perfect beau for her lovelorn friend Joan. I did not disagree, thinking that a date with a young doctor sounded frightfully romantic.

It turned out that the brother had a couple of tickets for a dance on Saturday evening, and thought that the ideal prologue to this would be a leisurely row up the river in the afternoon. Sounded pretty good to me!

Saturday arrived and, amid much banter from Fiz about my becoming Mrs Twittington-Hoggins (which was jumping the gun a bit, though I suppose it would have been better than Rigor Mortis), I got myself ready for the date of my dreams: make-up, perfume, brightest dress, the lot – I was leaving nothing to chance.

Giggling like two schoolgirls, Fiz and I placed ourselves discreetly by the flat window high above the Bayswater Road, looking out over the street. I was working myself up into a state of high excitement at the prospect of a new man in my life, and my anticipation increased as we scanned every visible single young male driving up and parking his car. Was it that tall and slender hunk strolling towards us puffing on his pipe? No: he turned and started walking in the opposite direction. Was it that gorgeous dark-haired soldier? No: *he* went into the building next door.

Just as I was beginning to think I was going to be stood up on my blind date, a car drew up and parked across the road – and out of it climbed Neanderthal Man. His complexion was swarthy, his hair hadn't seen a comb for weeks, and the crotch of his trousers was about down to his kneecaps. No, no – please God, no! – but as we watched in horror he glanced up at our building and strode across the road.

We heard the lift moving up from the ground floor and stopping outside our door.

Please don't let the bell ring! Please don't let the bell ring! – but it did, and a moment later this grisly specimen (no offence) was standing in the flat and introducing himself.

Fiz could hardly contain herself, but managed to squeeze out a 'Have a nice time' as my date and I went out the door – and she says she can still picture my frightened face peering imploringly out of the little window of the lift at her, then disappearing downwards and out of sight.

We drove to the river at Hampton Court and hired a rowing boat. My spirits rose a bit: at least I'd get to lounge in the back while Neanderthal

Man showed off his muscle power and rowed me along. But he had other ideas, and suggested that I take the oars for the first part of our trip. As he proceeded to settle himself in the stern and started sipping whisky from the hip flask he'd brought along, I rolled up the sleeves of my dress, grasped the oars and rowed. I rowed all the way up to Richmond, then turned the boat around and started rowing back. I'd understood that he was to take over the oars well before now, but he showed little inclination: surely he'd do the proper thing for the return leg?

Not a bit of it. Instead, he carried on lying in the rear of the boat, one hand dangling lazily over the side and into the water while the other kept putting the hip flask to his lips – the hip flask which he never once offered to me.

'Ah, this is the life, by Jove,' he sighed, 'this is the life!'

You may imagine how well that went down at my end of the boat.

Halfway back, when I'd heard him pronounce, 'This is the life!' for about the twentieth time, I downed oars.

He seemed startled: 'Oh – shall I take over now?'

'I think you'd better. I'm knackered!' – and so my gallant escort rowed us back to Hampton Court.

Going on to the dance was out of the question. The situation called for drastic action – and a bit of emergency acting. I suddenly remembered that I had another appointment that evening, and went to the nearest phone box. While Neanderthal Man waited outside, I picked up the handset, discreetly placed my finger over the button, and spoke into the mouthpiece, to the thin air: 'Hallo, it's Joan . . . Yes, of course I'm still coming, but I'm running a little late . . . I've been having such a wonderful time I couldn't drag myself away . . . Yes . . . I'll be there are soon as I can . . . Bye!'

I offered profuse apologies to my escort and asked him to drive me back to the flat.

End of The Blind Date From Hell – and end of any helping hand from Fiz, thank you very much. From then on I'd be finding my own escorts.

Late in 1953 several members of the *High Spirits* team were reunited at the New Lindsey for a new revue called *More Intimacy at Eight*, written by Peter Myers, Alec Grahame and David Climie, with music by John Pritchett and Ronnie Cass. In April 1954, after a try-out in Brighton, the show transferred to the Criterion Theatre as *Intimacy at 8.30*, with a cast consisting of five men (Geoffrey Hibbert, Ronnie Stevens, Digby Wolfe, Ron Moody and Peter Felgate) and four women (Joan Heal, Dilys Laye, Fiz and myself), with Aud Johansen as compere. (When Dilys and Geoffrey left the company to join the cast of *The Boy Friend* in New York, they were replaced by Hugh Paddick and Stephanie Voss.)

We made a great team, and there was inevitably a fair amount of banter among us. Digby Wolfe was a notorious woman-chaser, and before we went on stage one night I waited until I knew he would be changing into his costume for the opening number – then walked straight into the dressing room without knocking. My timing was perfect: he was absolutely starkers.

'Oh Digby,' I said, looking at the appropriate place, 'is that what all the fuss is about?'

I don't think he ever forgave me.

The understudies for *Intimacy at 8.30* included Edward Woodward – who took over one of the male leads when a production of the revue went to Germany to entertain the British forces out there – and Janet Deely. One afternoon Joan Heal had gone to the cinema to see *Doctor in the House*, and after a while along came the scene in which Dr Sparrow tries to chat up Nurse Rigor Mortis, played by . . .

'Oh God!' yelled Joan to the person sitting next to her. 'What day is it?'

'Wednesday.'

'Wednesday? Oh God, oh God!' – and she was out of her seat like a shot.

She tore along to the theatre, arriving just in time for her star number, a patter song called 'Peter Patter' which she performed with Geoffrey Hibbert. Janet Deely had been coping wonderfully in her absence, and no one alerted Geoffrey to the fact that Joan had arrived – so he got the shock of his life when she, rather than Janet, strode on to the stage and launched straight into the patter.

*Intimacy at 8.30* was directed by Michael

Charnley, whose style with actors ranged along a scale which stretched from brutal at one end to vicious at the other. Despite my RADA training, nature had never intended me to be a lithe and lissom ballet dancer, and when rehearsing *Intimacy* at the New Lindsey I sometimes had difficulty picking up my steps. But I could have done without Michael bellowing at me: 'Oh, for God's sake, stop moving around the stage like a bloody great carthorse!'

The show was a big hit, running at the Criterion for seventeen months – success which Ronnie Cass has suggested to me had a good deal to do with the show's title: 'We were a pretty prudish lot in those days, and all those coachloads of farmers coming up from the country for a night on the town probably thought they were in for something saucy with a show called *Intimacy*.'

It was during the run of *Intimacy* that I went to the hairdresser's for what should have been a perfectly straightforward hairdo – but they failed to dilute the peroxide and applied it neat. I left the hairdresser's looking like a bouffant canary. That afternoon I went to the cinema with a boyfriend. Halfway through the film my scalp started to itch like mad, and when I put my hand up to scratch it I found that it was weeping. My head was melting! As soon as I got home I washed my hair over and over again, and eventually the itching eased; but after a few days the problem had spread to my face, which came up in blotches – highly unsightly, and though make-up could mask my condition during a performance, the whole business left me feeling extremely low.

One night after we had come off stage Bill Linnit, of Linnit and Dunfee, the management company behind *Intimacy*, came into my dressing room just after I had taken off my make-up. He took one look at the blotches on my face and insisted that I consult – at his expense – a Harley Street doctor he knew: although a general practitioner, Christopher Howard had a reputation for being a genius with skin problems. And indeed, after he'd worked his magic on me the problem never returned.

One of the great joys of revue was the need to keep the show fresh and topical, and we were often having to adapt our material just before going on stage in order to reflect a development in the news. One day when the pre-London tour was playing in Brighton, Lady Docker, the society hostess who furnished the gossip columnists with more material than any other individual of the time, paid a visit down a mine – presumably to cheer up the miners – and for that evening's performance an extra number was slipped in, with Joan Heal done up to the nines and dressed from head to foot in gold, intoning:

> Oh, it's fine down a mine
> It's divine down a mine . . .

The show also contained little 'black-out' sketches performed in front of the curtain while the scenery was being changed: I particularly liked the one where a monk and a nun came on, and the monk started singing:

> If you were the only girl in the world,
> And I were the only boy
> Nothing–

Black-out.

My own moment of glory in *Intimacy at 8.30* was that song of the frustrated *femme fatale* destined to exercise her charms as a station announcer – words by David Climie, music by John Pritchett – which had been introduced in *More Intimacy at Eight*. For this number I wore a very short skirt, a very tight sweater and high-heeled ankle-strap shoes, and the outfit was topped off with the sort of long, Veronica Lake-style blonde wig that I had worn in *The Belles of St Trinian's*. For additional effect I came up with the idea of removing the straps of my bra and replacing them with two lengths of elastic, so that my bust would gently and rather titillatingly bob up and down as I moved. Sexy, or what?

On my cue I tottered on to the stage and perched myself on a tall stool, then picked the microphone and spoke breathily into it:

> When I was young, the height of my ambition
> Was to be a thoroughgoing femme fatale . . .

I went on to describe how, at my enunciation of

'Woking . . . Woking', stokers would stop their stoking ('and lumps of coal drop from each nervous hand') and stockbrokers stop their broking – though the Lord Chamberlain's office, which vetted every show staged in the public theatre, demanded that we drop one couplet in the version submitted for approval, and I was not allowed to relate how poker players stop their poking.

My station announcing proved so irresistibly sexy that it even affected men of the cloth:

> I remember once a bishop and a graduate
>    collegian
> Just caught my voice as they were passing
>    through the Southern Region
> They were later found in Tunis, where they'd
>    joined the Foreign Legion,
> They were victims of the golden voice.

This song always went down a storm with audiences, though at one performance it proved rather too thoroughly provoking for a gentleman in the stalls. The number was going extremely well and I was hamming it up like nobody's business. In one of the verses around the middle of the song I'd just squeezed out the first 'Woking' when there came an impassioned cry of 'Oh, darling!' from the fourth row back. It was just as obvious to the rest of the audience as it was to me how far this man had succumbed to my fatal charms, and a hush fell over the auditorium. It remained there for the rest of the number, which I managed to struggle through despite my desperate embarrassment. There were no more laughs for 'Siren Song' that night.

This experience taught me the power performers can exert over their audiences, and although on this particular occasion that power might have gone too far and caused me (and doubtless the gentleman involved) embarrassment, I got a huge buzz from performing to a live audience. More than anything, enthusiasm from an audience satisfied my need to feel wanted: it was as if I was getting the adulation and appreciation that I felt had been denied me in childhood, and I wallowed in it.

But although I loved revue, I hated cabaret, one medium I was never able to crack. In revue you have the barrier of the footlights between you and the audience, whereas in cabaret you're right out there with them – and more often than not they're drunk, or munching their way through the bowl of nuts on the table, or nattering to their neighbour. I hated the fact that in cabaret you're open to abuse or heckling from certain elements, and I've never been much good at silencing a heckler with a quick retort. Having said all that against it, I do have one glowing memory of cabaret from around this time: playing at a hotel in Jersey, when Gracie Fields was topping the bill. She was a true star, and generous in the extreme: when we discovered that one of the songs in my act was also in hers, she insisted on taking it out of hers.

The railway child – at Station House and (*right*) with Aunt Floss, 'Aunt' Maud and my mother.

My twenty-first birthday – in rep in Luton.

Showing a leg in *The Happy Ha'penny* at the Citizens'
Theatre, Glasgow.

*Cameos:*

TOP: Getting all romantic with Dirk Bogarde in *Doctor in the House*.

Rank (courtesy Kobal)

BOTTOM: Enjoying a night at the flicks with Norman Wisdom in *Just My Luck*.

The hit revue *Intimacy at 8.30*: (*left to right*) Digby Wolfe, me, Peter Felgate, Aud Johansen, Eleanor Fazen, Ron Moody, Joan Heal and Ronnie Stevens. The Mander and Mitchensen Theatre Collection

A bevy of young lovelies with Tyrone Power in *Night of a Hundred Stars*: (*left to right*) Anna Massey, Peggy Cummings, Sheila Sim, me, Thelma Ruby, Brenda Bruce (*background*), Dulcie Gray (*foreground*) and Jean Kent.

Colombia, 1966: The Little White One declares 'Viva Cartagena!' – then take it away, South America!

Back to back for *The Dick Emery Show*.

*Carry On Larking*:

With the gang –
Charlie Hawtrey,
Kenny Williams,
Hattie Jacques, Sid
James, Jim Dale and
Barbara Windsor –
at Pinewood.

ABOVE: Director Gerry Thomas
being outrageous on the set of
*Don't Lose Your Head*.

LEFT: Cuddles with producer
Peter Rogers.

Gran with silly old moo Dandy Nichols in *Till Death Us Do Part*. BBC Picture Archives

Being presented to Princess Alexandra after a charity performance of *Jack and the Beanstalk* at the Richmond Theatre in 1984.

OVERLEAF:
Taking a break on the set of *One of Our Dinosaurs is Missing*.

For all my reservations about cabaret, of course, revue itself was not without its hitches (leaving aside the example of my over-enthusiastic admirer in the fourth row). Things could easily go wrong. On one occasion I completely forgot the words of 'Siren Song'. When you're speaking to a piano accompaniment you simply cannot stop – so I carried on the song in a sort of gibberish of cod-Welsh nonsense words until I managed to force my brain back to the real words and continue. Not much excess of audience enthusiasm that evening!

One excuse for my amnesia on that occasion could have been the arduous schedule we were working to during those months – eight shows a week on top of other commitments. If I was performing in revue in the evening and filming during the day, I'd have to subject myself to the kind of manic routine which is only manageable when you're young and fired with enthusiasm.

I'd get up at five in the morning, take a car to the studios (and it would be down to me to pay for it: being chauffeur-driven doesn't come until you're a star), spend the day filming, then take a car from the studio straight to the theatre, arriving by 'the half' (half an hour before curtain up) to prepare for the performance, perform and then go straight home to bed. There was no question of dancing into the early hours at Harry Green's when there was a film to be made the next day.

With that sort of timetable it's not surprising that occasionally we'd need a little boost to the system to keep up our energy levels, and often we'd take a pep pill in the form of a Purple Heart to give us a lift before going on stage. This was common practice in the theatre at the time.

The success of *Intimacy at 8.30* attracted all sorts of celebrities into the audience. Noël Coward had been to see us at the New Lindsey – he came backstage and gushed 'Marvellous evening! Simply marvellous!' in all directions – and Gene Kelly, one of the greatest of all song-and-dance men, then on the crest of his popularity after the release of *Singin' in the Rain* a couple of years earlier, came to see the show at the Criterion.

I performed on the same bill as Noël Coward in the Royal Variety Show at the London Palladium in November 1954, when we restaged 'The Shop Girl Princess' from *High Spirits*. The part which Ronnie Stevens had played at the Hippodrome was taken for the Royal Variety Show by an up-and-coming young comic named Frankie Howerd, who was constantly trying to grab the stage from me: he'd go so far into the footlights that I spent half the performance terrified that he was going to tumble into the audience.

The rest of the line-up featured some of the big stars of the day, including the great song-and-dance performer Jack Buchanan (with whom I would be appearing before long in the film *As Long as They're Happy*), Norman Wisdom, Bob Hope – and Noël, who performed three songs at breakneck pace and brought the house down.

After the show the cast was presented to the young Queen, which was a great thrill for me –

though hardly a greater one than the sheer excitement of being on the same bill as Noël Coward.

As soon as it was becoming apparent that *Doctor in the House* was a big hit at the box office, filming of a sequel was quickly scheduled.

In *Doctor at Sea* I was cast again as the Plain Jane character – Wendy, whose principal interests in life were eating, going to the cinema, and nabbing Dirk Bogarde as her husband. In this last endeavour I was at something of a disadvantage, as my rival in love was played by a young French actress appearing in her first English-speaking film. Her name was Brigitte Bardot.

Joan Sims versus Brigitte Bardot. I'll leave you to guess which of us got her man.

# 4

# Bacon and Eggs and Benzedrine

When the Rani of Sarawak decided that as her husband had gone to the trouble of buying her a flat overlooking Hyde Park she might as well make more use of it, I had to gather my belongings and depart. My old friend Pat Hornsby had returned to London to understudy Leslie Caron in *Gigi*, and together we found a top-floor flat (two twin-bedded bedrooms, £8 a week furnished) next to the Cavendish Hotel in Jermyn Street, just off Piccadilly.

The ensuing spell flat-sharing with Pat proved to be one of the happiest periods of my life, not least because we were extremely compatible. I have always been best at being second-in-command, at carrying out actions instigated by others, while Pat was brilliant at working out what needed to be done: she was a fantastic organiser. We were a good combination in other ways, too: for example, we both loved animals, and as soon as we could we got a pair of kittens.

Life in Jermyn Street, though, was not without its hairy moments.

Ian and David, old friends of Pat's from her childhood, were in London and needed somewhere to stay, and since there were plenty of beds in the flat we offered them one of the bedrooms while the pair of us moved into the other. We had a good meal and a few drinks, then we all turned in for the night.

Early the following morning we were still tucked up in our beds when the doorbell rang. It was three gentlemen from the landlord – the Cavendish Hotel next door – who had come round to check the drains: we'd forgotten we'd reported that the loo was playing up.

Panic! We rushed into the boys' room and woke them up with a hasty explanation of what was going on. Ian scarpered into the massive wardrobe that stood in the corner of the room, while David slid under the bed (presumably men examining the drainage wouldn't need to look under there) and Pat and I raced around tidying away their clothes and making their beds so that it would not look as if we'd had anybody there at all, let alone two strapping lads.

We'd just finished – as we thought – obliterating the evidence when one of the drainage experts came into that room, and proceeded to take a look around. Pat and I followed him in – and both froze as simultaneously we spotted, lying on the floor under the bedside table, a jockstrap. Pat distracted our visitor by pointing out something in the opposite corner of the room while I tried to kick the offending item under the bed. Have you ever tried dispatching a jockstrap with one neat kick? It's not as easy as you'd think, and I was frantically prodding away at this thing with my foot while Pat tried to keep the man's attention at the other end of the room. It was all very well playing in farces at the Aldwych: here we were in a real-life one, and any moment the wardrobe door might swing open and reveal . . .

But mercifully we just got away with it, and the landlord's representatives completed their tour of inspection none the wiser.

While Pat's mother Molly was staying with us I was invited to a gala evening at the Dorchester Hotel. I was extremely nervous about going to such a grand affair but determined to make the right impression, so I bought a long black dress, off the shoulder and very figure-hugging (quite like the dress I wore in the bar-room scenes in *Carry On Cowboy*), and on the afternoon of the big occasion paraded myself around the flat in this creation. Molly decided that the dress could be made even more figure-hugging – and proceeded to stitch me further into it just as I was about to leave. I might have looked the part, but such was the state of my excitement that I just had to spend a penny before setting off for the Dorchester. Try as I might, I simply couldn't get out of that ruddy dress. Molly had the answer: 'Just stand on the loo and pull it up' – which is exactly what I had to do.

Miles Eason, our neighbour downstairs, had been in the original production of *The Mousetrap*, but eventually resolved that an acting career was not for him. He decided to sell up in London and go and work in the world of antiques in, of all places, Venezuela, and before departing threw a huge farewell party, at which the walls of his flat were decorated with pound notes. (Miles was famous for his parties, at which the elegant actress Coral Browne regularly put the rest of us to shame by turning up looking absolutely stunning in some very simple but very expensive outfit. On one occasion she memorably told Myles Rudge that acting with Anthony Quayle 'is like acting with two tons of condemned veal'.)

Pat was away in Newcastle but I was determined to enjoy myself. After being the life and soul of the party into the early hours I was starting to wane, at which point Miles's flat-mate Michael came to my rescue – 'I'll find you something that'll make you feel better' – and gave me a tablet. Whoosh! I was off again, dancing and swigging champagne as if there were no tomorrow.

But there was, of course, and the day that was dawning was the day that Miles would be starting his journey to South America. Determined to help him in any way I could, I started madly sewing buttons on to his shirts in readiness for his trip – and when I started to wane again, Michael gave me another tablet. This kept me going until Miles finally departed at about one o'clock on the afternoon of the day after the party had started, and even when he had gone I still had an enormous amount of energy left – which I put to good use clearing up the debris, washing up and putting everything back in its place.

Then the effects of the tablets rapidly started wearing off – as is the way with Benzedrine – and suddenly I was feeling worse than I had ever felt in my life. I staggered back upstairs to our flat and lay on the sofa, feeling so ill that at first I simply did not know what to do. Everyone else who had been at the party had long gone, and I was in need of help. So I phone Peter Eade's wonderful assistant Laurena Dewar, who was working at the office not far away in Cork Street. When she heard what had happened she came straight over, cooked me a plate of steamed fish and mashed potato, stood over me while I ate it and put me to bed.

I'd learned another lesson.

It was at about this time that I took part in *Night of a Hundred Stars*, a midnight matinée at the London Palladium staged in order to raise funds for the Actors' Orphanage. The idea was to get together on one bill as many of the available stars in London as was possible, and one of the big numbers of the show was a song-and-dance routine featuring a chorus of girls supporting one of the greatest of Hollywood heart-throbs: Tyrone Power.

'Tall, dark and handsome' hardly begins to

104

capture the appeal of Tyrone Power – though he had all three characteristics in buckets. A mixture of Elvis Presley, Errol Flynn and Harrison Ford, he was so handsome it made me ache just to look at him – and I'd spent a good deal of my childhood doing just that, in the pages of *Picturegoer* or on the screen of the Radion in films like *Alexander's Ragtime Band*, *The Mark of Zorro* and *Jesse James*. No question: Tyrone Power was one of my all-time screen idols, and the chance to perform on stage with him was a real fulfilment of those girlish fantasies I'd indulged in back at Station House.

Tyrone Power's act in *Night of a Hundred Stars* was to be a full-blown, all-singing, all-dancing version of the song 'Chicago', and around the leading man was gathered a team of glamorous, high-kicking young lovelies including Sylvia Syms, Anna Massey (who insisted on asking the choreographer: 'What is my motivation?'), Jean Kent, Brenda Bruce, Thelma Ruby and myself. To a girl, we all doted on Ty (as he insisted we call him), but I felt especially honoured when he asked if I'd like to have dinner with him. I managed to squeeze out a 'Yes, I'd love to,' and before I knew it we were sitting in Scott's restaurant in Piccadilly nattering away as if we were old friends. He was the Hollywood superstar and I was just the chorus girl, but there was no side to him at all.

He was also (since you're no doubt wondering) the model of good manners, and I was such a greenhorn that although I found him devastatingly attractive it never crossed my mind that I would end up in the sack with him – which is just as well, as I didn't.

Ty then invited me to a dinner party at the house he was renting in Chester Street. This was a lovely occasion (I got deeply involved in conversation with the great actor Brian Aherne without realising who he was until much later!), and when at the end of the evening I went to say goodbye to Ty, he insisted on driving me home – in his 1935 Rolls-Royce, no less, registration number TP1.

As we approached Jermyn Street, I found myself thinking: If only Pat could see me now, being driven home in the early hours by Tyrone Power in his vintage Rolls-Royce . . .

He pulled up outside the flat, and before getting out of the car I said rather timidly, 'I really would love to be able to invite you round here, but I'm afraid all I could offer is bacon and eggs.'

'But I love bacon and eggs!' he replied – and with that he bade me goodnight and drove off.

I rushed up the stairs: 'Pat! Pat! You're not going to believe this! Tyrone Power's just brought me home in his vintage Rolls!' And for the next two hours Jermyn Street rang to the sound of girlish giggles as I told Pat every detail of a magical evening.

Gossip spreads like a bush fire in the theatre, and scarcely had I slipped into bed that night, still glowing with memories of a fantastic night out, than the rumour was whizzing around: Annabella was the first, Linda Christian was the second, and now Joan Sims is going to be the third Mrs Tyrone Power.

I'd taken Ty's protestation of love for bacon and eggs as no more than a characteristic piece of politeness from a famously chivalrous man, so I was amazed when a couple of days later I had a call from his manager, Bill Gallagher.

'Ty's really looking forward to coming round to your place for his bacon and eggs. Can we fix a date?'

Gulp.

'You mean he was serious?'

'Of course he was serious. When's it to be?'

Well, if Tyrone Power was really coming round for bacon and eggs we'd better make a proper evening of it, so I suggested to Bill that he come with Ty and we make up a foursome with Pat. It was all systems go.

When Miles Eason heard about our distinguished supper guests from the USA, he recommended that we serve a Caesar salad – whatever that was – alongside the bacon and eggs to make them feel at home; he even came up and showed me how to make it, bringing with him a salad bowl and the croutons.

After a great deal of nervous rushing around the flat as Pat and I dolled ourselves up, set the table, plumped the cushions and checked that Frank Sinatra's *Songs for Swinging Lovers* was on the turntable, Ty and Bill arrived.

I suggested that they make themselves comfortable in the sitting room while Pat and I finished off in the kitchen, but Ty insisted Pat stay and get to know Bill while he came and helped me prepare the food. He followed me into the kitchen, took off the jacket of his immaculate suit, put on a pinafore, rolled up the sleeves of his mono-grammed shirt and asked what he could do.

'Well, er . . . you could cut the rind off that bacon . . .'

So he set to work. This was an astonishing sight – Tyrone Power, man of my Hollywood dreams, standing beside me in my kitchen with his sleeves rolled up, cutting the rind off the bacon. I still sometimes wonder if it really happened.

Rind removed to perfection, the bacon was served up with the eggs and the Caesar salad. But it's not the taste of the food which formed the last-ing memory of that evening: it's the sound of *Songs for Swinging Lovers* being played over and over as two couples danced through the evening and long into the small hours.

Ty and Bill left about four in the morning, and Pat and I sat up until dawn, reliving the best supper party of our lives.

I saw Ty several times after that – for lunch or dinner – but in due course he had to return to the USA. A couple of weeks later I received a card from him: he'd loved the time we'd spent together in London, but he didn't want to get involved emotionally at that time, so we'd better not take it any further. I couldn't argue with that. It had been a lovely romantic interlude, and – like so much in my love life before and since – entirely innocent.

Not long after that card arrived I read that he had got married again, this time to a young American girl named Debbie Montgomery Minardos. They were expecting their first child when in November 1958 Ty had a heart attack on the set of *Solomon and Sheba* and died.

Tyrone Power cut the rind off my bacon. They can't take that away from me.

It was while I was living in Jermyn Street that I received some wildly exciting news. Gene Kelly had been so taken with *Intimacy at 8.30* when he'd been to see the show at the Criterion that he had raved about it to several New York producers, one of whom was intending to put on an American version in an off-Broadway theatre. The star would be Martha Raye, and just two of the English cast would go over and perform in the US version: Hugh Paddick (whom I affectionately called 'Huge Padlock') and myself.

I suppose my reaction to this was, looking back on it, a bit precipitate. I was terrified of flying, and knew that I'd have to cross the Atlantic by boat, so I went straight out and acquired the highest-quality cabin trunk that money could buy. It was absolutely typical of me to respond to a situation by tearing off and spending money on the best available gear. I'd done it with the kitchen equipment at the Adams' house in St John's Wood, and later on when I tried (briefly!) to learn golf I immediately bought an expensive set of clubs. Now I had this wonderful cabin trunk. I didn't have a formal agreement for the American run, mind you, but I did have the trunk.

Next I gave notice that I'd be leaving the Jermyn Street flat. Peter Eade did his best to calm me down ('Joan, the contract hasn't arrived – and you're not leaving these shores until all the legal stuff is signed and sealed'), but I wouldn't be told. I went on making plans for the trip: I was going to New York!

Then came the blow. The backers got cold feet about how well the show would adapt for US audiences, and the financial support was withdrawn. Peter Eade had been right, and I learned the hard way how deflating it can be to get too excited by a prospect before you know for sure that it will come off.

The worst aspect of this fiasco was that I was now not only jobless but homeless: I couldn't go back to Jermyn Street (Pat had already moved out, and the colonel who was the principal tenant of the flat was about to move back in), and I had nowhere else to go.

Desperate, I went to see the wonderful Miss Jeffery, manager at the Cavendish Hotel next door, and explained that I was without a home. She came to my rescue by allowing me to stay in a room in the staff accommodation at the back of the hotel – £2 10s a week, breakfast included – until I could find somewhere. In the event I was there several months before finding a flat above a chemist's shop in Wilton Place.

\* \* \*

The door to America had shut, but plenty of others had been opening. The arrival of commercial television in September 1955 had meant a significant increase in opportunities, and I was lucky enough to land two roles in the very earliest days of ITV. *Curtains for Harry*, transmitted in October 1955, was a one-hour one-off sitcom starring Bobby Howes as a music-hall performer who gets involved with some jewel thieves. My other early ITV appearances were in *Here and Now*, a weekly sketch show that ran from December 1955 to February 1956 and featured the likes of Ian Carmichael, Hugh Paddick and Nicholas Parsons. It was fun to work with them, but I was never very comfortable with performing revue material on television: somehow the one medium does not suit the other.

There was also radio. *Floggit's*, which was first broadcast in August 1956 and proved so popular that a second series was aired the following spring, starred Elsie and Doris Waters doing – well, doing their standard Elsie and Doris Waters routine: Gert and Daisy rambling on in the time-honoured manner. I played various bit parts – with names like Emma Smeed and Greta of the Red Lion – along with, among others, Ronnie Barker (the first time he was ever billed as 'Ronnie' rather than the more solemn Ronald), Hugh Paddick and Anthony Newley. Ronnie and Tony got the sack after the first series as Elsie and Doris felt they were taking too many laughs from themselves, and the show subsequently featured other familiar names in Ron Moody and John Junkin.

But I already knew that the cinema was where I most wanted to make my mark – and, happily, the roles kept pouring in. Many of those early films are completely forgotten now (even by me), but they gave me the opportunity to work with some of the great names, and names didn't come much greater at the time than the star of *As Long as They're Happy*: Jack Buchanan. I'd love to be able to tell how I performed a glitzy song-and-dance routine with him, but I was still very much at the stage of grabbing every decent cameo role I could get, and was just the fainting maid, overcome by the sight of the big Hollywood star turning up in the household. (Years later a fan asked me: 'Do you always play these falling-down parts?' and when I thought back, I suppose she was right; I certainly played a good many falling-down parts in those early days.)

*Dry Rot* was the film version of a popular theatrical farce about bookmakers staging some sort of betting coup, and starred Brian Rix, Ronnie Shiner, Sid James and Peggy Mount. It was directed by Maurice Elvey, who could be very autocratic – as poor Michael Shepley found out during the filming of one scene which involved a good deal of going out of one door and in through another. It was a very complex piece of manoeuvring, and unsurprisingly, given the amount of business which involved doors being opened with split-second timing, all signalled by cue lights, things had started to go a bit wrong technically. With each successive take Maurice was getting more and more frantic and Michael more and more flustered, and in the end Maurice's patience snapped. He shouted at Michael: 'Oh, do come along, we must get this right now; we've wasted about half an hour's screen time.' Bellowing like that is the last thing you do to an actor when things are going wrong, and Sid James decided it was time to make a point. He announced that he was leaving the set until Maurice apologised to Michael for that outburst, and off he strode. Maurice duly apologised and no more was said, but I was hugely impressed by the stand Sid took.

In June 1956 I opened at the Aldwych in *Man Alive*, a farce written by John Dighton and directed by Billie Chappell, very much in the tradition of the Ben Travers plays which in the 1920s and 1930s had been synonymous with that theatre. *Man Alive* was set in the front window of a department store, whose manager was played by that wonderful actor Robertson Hare. 'Bunny', immortalised in his catchphrase 'Oh, calamity!', had first made his name in Ben Travers farces in the 1920s and was still one of the funniest comic actors around.

In the window were two dummies – a sophisticated adult one played by Joan Benham and a child dummy, named Jubilee, played by myself. Dressed in a little frock, frilly petticoat, ankle socks and black patent-leather strapped shoes, I was carried on to the stage at the beginning of the first act by David Evans, playing one of the shop assistants, and plonked down – and had to remain there, totally immobile, unless my position was altered by one of the 'live' actors. I wasn't to move even so much as an eyelid, and one of the abiding memories of rehearsals is of our director Billie Chappell exhorting us: 'Now try not to blink, darlings!'

Knowing that I could do nothing to resist, David Evans took advantage of my immobility: every evening as he brought me on, he'd fiddle about making sure my knickers were straight or otherwise adjusting my clothing. There Joan and I stayed – me on one side of the stage, she on the other, exchanging dialogue which the humans couldn't hear – until the cramp or pins and needles became unbearable, at which point we'd issue a prearranged signal to one of the others to come to our rescue: a low murmuring noise ('Mmmmmmmmmm') would usually be enough to bring the relief of another actor altering the position of a leg or an arm.

But the real problem was when the unexpected happened during a performance.

For one Wednesday matinée there was a very thin house, and by the third act – most of which I spent astride a kiddies' tricycle, Joan and I both having been brought on wrapped from head to toe in brown paper – the few old dears in the audience were more concerned with clinking their cups and saucers than with what was taking place on the stage. Early in the act Marjorie Dunkels, playing a rather masculine lady shopper, stormed on demanding to see the store manager, at which point two old ladies in the audience, who had spent most of the play chattering to each other, paused in their conversation. Then one turned to the other:

'What is it, dear – a man or a woman?'

Her friend considered for a moment, then replied:

'I don't know, dear, but I shouldn't think it matters much.'

Sitting motionless astride my tricycle, I heard this exchange clearly, and a second later was madly trying to stifle my laughter. I clutched the handle-bars as tightly as I could until they started vibrating, and knew that if I glanced across at Joan I'd be done for – so I just sat there desperately trying to get control of myself. I managed to, but it was a near thing.

Not much chance for grace and charm of movement in that role!

My next theatre part was in *Breath of Spring* by Peter Coke. First staged at the Theatre Royal, Nottingham, in March 1958, it opened in London at the Cambridge Theatre later that month and transferred to the Duke of York in August, running through to April the following year.

In this production I again encountered the legendary comic actress Athene Seyler, whose dislike of A. A. Milne and all his works had done me such a bad turn at my first RADA audition a decade earlier. She was a delight to work with, and for me as a young actress learning the trade it was fascinating to watch Athene's way of playing comedy: her timing was exquisite, her double takes and the looks she used to throw to the audience judged to perfection.

Not only was working with her an education in itself, she was exceptionally kind to me. For no apparent reason, I started to get very hung up over the phrase 'petty falsehood' in my first scene with Athene. This is not uncommon with actors, but it can prove very undermining, as words can lose all meaning if you think about them over and over and over, and the more I worried about this phrase, the more it seemed to be a completely meaningless sequence of letters. I started to think that the audience would be saying to themselves: 'What's she saying that nonsense for? It means nothing!' Once you start to think like this you're on very dangerous ground, as every time you play that scene you feel like a rider approaching a jump, nervous about getting over it. At first you just hesitate and squeeze the words out, but things can get worse, and in this case my delivery of the crucial line was disintegrating into a sort of stammer.

At this stage *Breath of Spring* had been running for about six months, and I put the problem down – in part, at least – to what I call Long Run Doom – the point in a show's run where you know your lines backwards and have become over-familiar with the material.

Suddenly it was as if I was back in Chorlton-cum-Hardy with my panic over *Sarah Simple*, but with no Mrs Spreckley to come to my rescue. I mentioned my problem to Athene, who was wonderfully sympathetic.

'The trouble is that you've been doing this play for a long time, and the words are losing their meaning for you. Come to my dressing room at the ten' – meaning ten minutes before curtain up – 'and we'll look at that speech together.' I did so, and Athene said it was simply a matter of speaking that line – and especially those two words – as if I were doing so for the very first time. Since I'd spoken the ruddy phrase about three thousand times that was easier said than done, but a combination of Athene's limitless patience and the old trick of writing the words in big capital letters on a piece of cardboard and staring at it for minutes on end to burn it on to my brain, repeating it over and over, saw me through.

The immediate problem was resolved, but already I was finding the stage a less congenial medium than film, television or radio. Part of the problem was that I never liked long runs. It was, of course, lovely to be in a successful play, to have the excitement of performing a hit to packed houses (and, not least, the assurance of a regular income for the foreseeable future). But on the other hand, I found it extremely difficult to keep a performance fresh, and I'd soon get bored. That's why filming is so exhilarating: every day brings something different, a fresh adrenalin flow.

Playing the policeman in *Breath of Spring* was Tony Baird, a very experienced stage actor who had appeared in many West End productions, and in due course he and I became very close – a relationship which proved to be something of a mixed blessing.

When I first knew Tony I couldn't bear him. From a Scots background, he was the elder of two brothers, and while his younger brother Simon was the very successful manager of a hotel, Tony himself was something of the black sheep of the family. I never wanted too many details of why he was so cast, but he definitely had a reputation for being a bit of rogue, and he did not do much to try to play that reputation down. The old chemistry soon started to work, and I found myself beginning to like him – and before I knew it I was madly in love.

I was in my late twenties, Tony in his early forties and divorced. After we had been dating for a while he moved in with me at the little flat I was renting in Wilton Place, and for the first time in my life I experienced the satisfaction not only of what felt like my first real romance, but of a long-term, close, loving relationship.

Like any young girl I'd developed terrific crushes on men I'd met at parties, but I was always useless at flirting, and simply did not know what needed to be done in order to snare my target. If I felt the vibes coming from him I'd come over all shy, and when I saw other girls giving a man the come-on I'd think: I wish I could do that. I always ended up resorting to jokes, and most men don't like funny women. *They* like to do the jokes.

Although Tony and I would have been free to marry, we never even discussed it, and the idea of settling down and having a family didn't cross our minds. Rather, we spent our spare time in the usual pursuits – cinema, friends, good food and swelling the coffers of the Nag's Head in Kinnerton Street. We had a very settled and relaxed relationship, and our closeness survived even my horror at discovering that Tony's pride and joy, his boat moored on the Thames at Chiswick, was little more than a peeling wreck.

Had househusbands been in vogue in those days we'd have made an excellent couple, since Tony was not very successful as an actor and I soon became the main breadwinner. If we had been able to accept that I would go out and earn the money and he would concentrate on running the home, things might have turned out better.

We managed quite happily for a couple of years, but then the dark cloud on the horizon that had slowly been coming nearer and nearer was suddenly overhead.

In those days 'living in sin' was considered just that – a profoundly immoral way to behave. If you were married, you lived with your partner; if you were not, you did not. Even within the occasionally socially unorthodox world of the stage it was pretty unusual for unmarried couples to live together, and the only couple I knew who were cohabiting were Kenneth More and Angela Douglas: I often found myself wishing I had Angela's guts and could be more open about my relationship with

Tony, but I felt too guilty, and spent a great deal of time doing my best to conceal the fact.

The only two people with whom I could discuss our situation in the knowledge that we had their support were our downstairs neighbours Horace (Holl) Godman and his wife Bill (short for Lillian). 'As long as you're happy, that's all that matters,' went Bill's constant attempts at reassurance, and I took a good deal of strength from their understanding. They had no children, and tended to look on me as a kind of daughter. The trouble was, of course, that I was already someone else's daughter, and eventually I knew that telling my parents the true extent of my wickedness could be put off no longer.

It all came to a head one Christmas after Tony and I had been living together for about two years. He had wanted me to stay up in London with him over the Christmas period but I knew that I had to go down to Essex, where, following my father's retirement from the LMS Railway, I had bought my parents a house in Southchurch.

As an only child, it was out of the question for me to stay away from home at that time of the year, and although it meant a great deal of play-acting when I was there, that was simply how it had to be. But I was getting fed up with leading a double life – keeping my happiness with Tony a secret from my parents, and in turn not revealing to him the full horror of how my mother would react if she knew – and I knew that the deception could not go on for ever.

I travelled down to Essex a few days before Christmas. My mother knew that something was going on in my life – she wasn't stupid – and knew that I was involved in some way with Tony; but she did not know (or, more probably, did not want to know) just how deeply. To her, whose overriding principle in life remained 'You can always stoop and pick up nothing', I deserved better, and should have been content to keep myself in readiness for the Mr Perfect who was surely out there somewhere, rather than throw myself away on this fellow. She had never met Tony, but did not let that detail prejudice her: he was not fit for her Joan, and there was an end to it.

The problem was that it was by no means an end to it, and as soon as I'd arrived in Essex she started letting slip provocative remarks like: 'I hope you're not still with that chap Tony. He's been married before, you know.' I bit my lip and let her move on to one of her regular themes: 'There's nothing in sex, you know, nothing at all: I don't know what all the fuss is about.'

She carried on niggling away and I carried on ignoring her: I had no intention of demolishing the family Christmas by revealing all.

But then, on the evening of the day before Christmas Eve, I was with her in the kitchen while my father was in the living room listening to the radio, and as I nattered away about life in London she went back to making her derogatory little comments. I'd had a drink or two (after all, it was Christmas, and the sherry was being given its annual outing), and gradually my resistance was eroded.

Deep breath.

'Mummy, I have to tell you. Tony has been living with me for two years. I'm very happy, and you'll just have to accept it.'

Deathly silence, and then the floodgates burst. She rushed in to my father, yelling: 'John! John! Do you know what our daughter has just told me? She's living in sin with that man!'

There was a pause which seemed to go on for ever. Then my father said calmly: 'Well, Gladys, I suppose we can't expect our daughter to lead the life of a nun' – and with that single comment he turned and went upstairs to bed.

The wailing and lamentation continued (I could see where the actress in me had come from), and try as I might to reason with her and talk the matter through in an adult way – I was not far off thirty, for heaven's sake! – she wouldn't listen. Eventually she too went up to bed, and after a couple more drinks to try to calm myself, I did the same.

My father was sleeping in a bedroom at the back of the house, and my mother and I had the twin beds in a room at the front. I'd been hoping that she would have gone to sleep by the time I went up, but no such luck. She was lying there sobbing, and my joining her in the bedroom just made things worse. All night the wailing went on, and neither of us got any sleep at all.

In the morning I told her, as gently as I could,

that if she was going to go on sobbing for the rest of Christmas then I'd have to go back to London. She had to accept that Tony had made me very happy and that he should be welcomed as part of the family, and if she could not do that, then I couldn't stay. She just lay there with her face turned to the wall, and made no reply.

Then I went into my father's room to tell him what had happened. All he could say was: 'This is going to break your mother's heart, you know.'

So I drove back to London. I was desolated by the whole experience, but I knew that I was doing the right thing.

A few days later, just after Christmas, a letter arrived at Wilton Place. It was in my father's handwriting, but the words were certainly my mother's: 'Fingers of shame will be pointing at you .... Remove this seducer from your home ... God knows how you have persecuted us.' It went on in the same vein for four pages.

I was dumbstruck. The only person I could approach for advice was Peter Eade, by then much more a mentor and friend than just my agent. 'You've got to write back,' he said; so I did, saying that persecuting them was the very last thing in the world I wanted to do, but that they had to come to terms with the fact that Tony was an extremely important part of my life – and if they could not, then we'd have to go our separate ways.

The letter was duly posted to Southchurch. I never had a reply, and for the next six months or so I had no contact with my parents whatsoever.

It would be nice to able to report that these ructions made me closer to Tony, and that we then settled down and lived happily ever after, but sadly I can't. The terrible episode with my parents just underlined my own guilt, which in turn brought a background of tension to my life with Tony.

Little – and not so little – things started to annoy me. I started to realise that I was financing him much more than was right. He had jobs in the theatre but I was still the breadwinner, and this began to grate. Nothing he tried ever seemed to work out. He applied to be a taxi driver, even going so far as doing 'The Knowledge' and learning all the streets of London. But he never got as far as actually getting his cabbie's licence, so that avenue was closed off. If he came by some money, he'd buy me a present and then go down to the Nag's Head and buy a round for everybody. Most of all he wanted to be an actor – he once said to me, 'Even at the risk of losing you, I have to be an actor' – but he was never good enough to make it in that world.

For three years I was besotted with this lovable reprobate, but then the icing on the cake began to chip off, and the love started to wear thin. I was virtually keeping him, and the friction of the situation was getting ever harder to bear.

The straw that finally broke the camel's back came on my return from a tour. Tired after a long trip away, I went into the flat and made straight for the bathroom to dump my washing in the linen basket. In the basket I found a dozen dirty shirts. I hit the roof: I'd been working, and all he'd been doing was sitting around with his feet up or propping up the bar in the Nag's Head. I'd been on bloody tour, bloody well earning all the bloody money – couldn't he even have gone to the bloody launderette?

It was a minor incident, of course, but from then on things started to peter out, and one night I came back from that evening's performance and told him that we couldn't carry on. He had to move out. It was awful – and more awful the following night when I came back from the theatre: he was slumped in the armchair looking through the rented property columns of the *Evening Standard*. I could tell that he was genuinely heartbroken, and so was I, but I had to do it for my own survival.

After Tony came John Walters, whom I had known for ages. He'd been assistant stage manager for *High Spirits* and we'd had an innocent little romance back then, but nothing developed at the time. Now, as my feelings for Tony waned, so I became more interested in John, and not very long after Tony moved out of Wilton Place, John moved in.

John, who had been brought up in a children's home, was much more moody than Tony had been, and somehow I never felt that ours would be a long-term relationship: I simply couldn't have lived permanently with those wildly varying changes in his temperament. At one point we did talk of getting married and having children – the only time I have ever thought seriously about it –

but we agreed that we both had too many reservations. I was going through the one and only broody phase of my life; but it didn't last, and I've never been able to understand women who have this burning desire to have children. I've simply never had those feelings in any depth: maybe I should have realised that I would never be very maternal when I was boring holes into my dolls' stomachs with my father's screwdriver.

John and I parted after about two years' living together.

The fact that I – whose screen presence has not exactly played down the idea of being attractive to men – have never married seems to have baffled some people (it's even listed as an interesting fact about Joan Sims on a website devoted to me!), but to me there's no great mystery. I never married because the right person never came along. Tony was not the right man. John was not the right man. Nor was anyone else. I leave others to seek for darker explanations. For me it's extremely simple!

The rift with my parents and the subsequent problems with Tony made for a very sombre time; but the show must go on, and film parts continued to come in – mostly cameo roles for silly blonde girls. *Just My Luck*, my second film with Norman Wisdom, saw me at my blondest and silliest as the girl whom an over-enthusiastic gambler takes out to the flicks in the hope of getting his hands on the pound note in her handbag. There was all sorts of comic business in the cinema stalls, with Norman trying to kiss me and getting all mixed up and kissing the old man behind instead – very much the standard Norman Wisdom fare at the time, and very successful. About all I can remember about it now is that there was a great deal of mauling going on, with me being terribly upright and prim.

*The Naked Truth*, a very funny and sadly underrated film in which Dennis Price as editor of a scandal sheet tries to blackmail celebrities played by Peter Sellers (in a wonderful array of disguises), Terry-Thomas, Shirley Eaton and Peggy Mount, proved a real breakthrough, for my role as Ethel Ransom, daughter of one of the victims (the detective-story writer played by Peggy Mount), moved me out of cameo roles and gave me more to get my teeth into.

It also proved a move away from my standard flimsy blonde. I dyed my hair dark brown and became a very twittery girl overruled by her domineering mother. It was a wonderful part to play, and a wonderful experience to be working with some of the finest comic actors around. I really threw myself into that role, and discovered the extraordinary effect of having my hair dyed. It quite transformed my character, toning down my whole personality, shrinking me into that very nervous, very mousy little me needed for the role. But at the end of the film I couldn't wait to be blonde again, and washed the dye out as soon as I could.

*The Naked Truth* was directed by Mario Zampi, one of the kindest directors I ever worked with –

very Italian, very *simpatico* – and one day towards the end of filming he asked me if I had any holiday plans after we'd finished. When I replied that I hadn't, he insisted that I accompany his wife Kitty to Italy for the three weeks he'd be editing the film, and then he'd come out and join us. This was not an offer to refuse. Kitty and I spent a marvellous time luxuriating in a hotel in the middle of a pine forest; then Mario joined us – somewhat later than originally planned – and insisted on paying for me from then on, since his delay had caused me to run out of money. We moved on to Rome, where the Hotel Excelsior on the Via Veneto was our base for one of the most enjoyable weeks I'd ever spent – much of it enjoyed in the extremely jolly company of Mario's mother and his lovely chubby brother Nando. Although I'm not one of life's great sight-seers, it was thrilling to be shown around the Eternal City by Mario, and somewhat less thrilling to be goosed by a priest in St Peter's, though I suppose that's all part of the fun of being a tourist in Italy.

Mario died in 1963. He was a great film-maker, and a good friend to me.

As far as my career was concerned, I was clearly now a leading choice for certain sorts of roles in certain sorts of films, and I was very happy about the way things were going. So I hardly paid much attention when in August 1958 a cheap-and-cheerful film made at Pinewood Studios, produced by Peter Rogers, directed by Ralph Thomas's brother Gerald and featuring several actors I had worked with (William Hartnell, Shirley Eaton, Ken

128

Connor and Hattie Jacques among them), was
released upon an unsuspecting world.
It was called *Carry On Sergeant*.

# 5

# Just Another Film

The story of how a group of raw recruits in the army excel themselves and win the Star Squad award, *Carry On Sergeant* had little about it to suggest that it would become a landmark in British cinema. Although it featured a few actors I knew, I did not go to see it in the cinema and it made little impression on me.

It made plenty of impression at the box office, however, and struck such a nerve with the cinema-going public that in the autumn of 1958 Peter Rogers and Gerald Thomas started to plan a sequel. This was to be called *Carry On Nurse*, and Peter Eade got a call from the casting director: was I available? I was, and in November 1958 I went down to Pinewood to begin filming what would prove to be the first of my twenty-four *Carry On*s.

At the time it felt like just another film, but there was definitely, even at that very early stage, a real camaraderie and sense of fun about the whole team – cast and crew – which was not always present in other films I had worked in.

As with *Sergeant*, the screenplay for *Carry On Nurse* was written by Norman Hudis, and, as with the earlier film, it milked the comic possibilities of life within an institution: first the army, now a large general hospital. Whether my appearance in *Life in Emergency Ward Ten* had me marked down as ideal material for nursing roles I have no idea, but in *Carry On Nurse* I was cast as the young student nurse Stella Dawson, playing alongside actors who were to become *Carry On* regulars, including Hattie Jacques, Kenneth Williams (whom I had met in Peter Eade's office but could not claim to know well), Charles Hawtrey and Kenneth Connor.

Stella Dawson is a very innocent addition to the nursing ranks, as is obvious from her attempt to have patient Ted York (Terence Longden) take a suppository by mouth – 'Other end, Nurse!' instructs a passing senior. 'Never mind,' Longden reassures the embarrassed Nurse Dawson. 'With a face like mine it's a mistake anyone might make.' But by the end she is confident enough to join in the prank staged against the Colonel, a difficult patient played by Wilfred Hyde-White.

Stella Dawson and another nurse tell the Colonel that they have to take his temperature, setting up the final scene of the film. When the Matron (Hattie Jacques) enters the Colonel's room she is taken aback to find him lying on his stomach, pyjama trousers pulled down and an object sticking out of his rear end.

131

'Come come, Matron,' he explains. 'Surely you've seen a temperature taken like this before!'

'Yes, Colonel, many times – but never with a daffodil.'

Not only was *Nurse* my first *Carry On*, it was also the first time – but not the last – that I shed blood for the series. A piece of comic business had me rushing out of a room into the corridor just as a surgical trolley was being wheeled past. The resulting collision – Joan Sims in a falling-down part yet again – may have raised a few laughs in the cinema, but it didn't do much for me: the sharp edge of the trolley left a deep gash in my shin, and I was rushed off to the Pinewood medical room. It was not much consolation to me, as I lay there having stitches sewn into the wound, that the take had been given the OK, and my injury had not caused any hold-up. Then – as always – the *Carry On* films were shot on an extremely tight schedule, and there was no time to lie around feeling sorry for myself: I was back on the set shooting another scene before the end of the day.

By the end of 1959 *Carry On Nurse* had made a serious commercial impact and was the biggest box-office hit in Britain that year. It was also to prove a huge success in the USA. But as far as I was concerned Stella Dawson was simply another part; there were plenty of other roles keeping me busy.

I still seemed to be specialising in cameo roles, but had no objection to that, as a succession of short appearances in several different films would serve as a useful showcase for my ability to play different characters – often more than one in the same film. In *Please Turn Over*, directed by Gerald Thomas and starring Ted Ray, Leslie Phillips and Charles Hawtrey, I played two roles: the French maid, and a cleaning lady with a fag constantly hanging out of her mouth. Such versatility! In *The Captain's Table* I worked again with John Gregson. *Upstairs and Downstairs*, produced by Betty Box, directed by Ralph Thomas and featuring Michael Craig, James Robertson Justice, Daniel Massey, Claudia Cardinale and Sid James, got me in the wars again when a piece of comedy business which involved falling over a suitcase left me laid up with a bruised leg. I did not think too much about this at the time, and in any case there was another *Carry On* in the offing: I was to play the gym mistress, Miss Sarah Allcock, in *Carry On Teacher*.

By the time we'd been filming *Teacher* for a couple of weeks, the pain in my leg was getting worse. Arriving at the studio one day I decided that it was so bad I had to pay a visit to the first aid unit, where I was told that I had a thrombo-phlebitis in my right leg and should take it very easy indeed. For the rest of that day's shooting I worked with my leg propped up on a chair out of sight of the camera. It always amuses me to see those shots whenever *Teacher* is shown on the tele-vision – sweet Miss Allcock looking so fit and hearty, and only I knew that her gammy leg was propped up just out of sight. At the end of the day's filming it was arranged that I could be whisked off to hospital, where I had to remain for about ten days. The filming schedule had to be revamped, but Peter Rogers and Gerry Thomas were always wonderful about rearranging things if any of their actors got into difficulties. Peter famously said, 'I'll do anything for my actors except pay them,' but we'll come to that matter later . . .

Miss Allcock was a great role to play, but she was very nearly not Miss Allcock at all. When the screenplay was submitted to the Lord Chamberlain's office, concern was expressed about the name, and it was decreed that it could only be pronounced with equal stress on each of the two syllables. Try telling that to the besotted child psychologist Alistair Grigg, played with drooling passion by Leslie Phillips: his yearning pronunciation of 'Miss Allcock' was more heavily charged than anything the Lord Chamberlain could have dreamed of.

*Carry On Teacher* gave me some hugely enjoyable scenes – such as the drunken fight in the staff-room with the haughty school inspector Felicity Wheeler (played by Rosalind Knight, one of Peter Eade's first clients), the itching powder episode or the split gym shorts – as well as some typical early *Carry On* innuendo. Take, for example, Miss Allcock's conversation with Alistair Grigg and Felicity Wheeler during a session in the gym:

*Felicity Wheeler*: Are you satisfied with your equipment?

*Miss Allcock*: Well, I've had no complaints so far.
*Alistair Grigg*: Do you find mental relaxation follows physical activity?
*Miss Allcock*: Oh, always.
*Felicity Wheeler*: Do you favour the Swedish method?
*Miss Allcock*: Well, I always say it's the same the whole world over.

Driven along by that sort of harmless double meaning, the *Carry On* formula was proving highly popular, and two more films followed in quick succession.

*Carry On Constable*, which we started filming in November 1959, was a take-off of *Dixon of Dock Green* featuring Kenneth Williams, Kenneth Connor and Leslie Phillips as young constables sent to a police station where the staff has been hit by a flu epidemic. There they are joined by Charles Hawtrey as PC Timothy Gorse, who insists on bringing his budgerigar Bobby on duty with him. The sergeant at the police station was Sid James – Sid's first *Carry On* part – and I played WPC Gloria Passworthy, the pursuit of whom by the timorous and superstitious Constable Constable (Ken Connor) provided the romantic interest.

An unexpected technical problem cropped up when we were filming the scene in which the four constables are taking a shower. They discover that the water is running cold, and rush out of the shower-room clad only in towels. When the scene was first filmed, the reflection from those four bare

135

bottoms caused a 'flare' in the camera, which ruined the shot. Make-up man George Blackler was sent for, and the rest of us hung around while George put each of the actors on a trestle table and proceeded to apply powder to the offending areas, mumbling all the while about how he'd made up Margaret Lockwood and dozens of other stars, but this was the first time he'd had to make up a bum! But it did the trick: no more flaring, and the scene remains a great favourite among *Carry On* fans.

The next in the series was *Carry On Regardless*, the story of how a group of out-of-work men and women take on various odd-job assignments for the Helping Hands agency. Kenneth Williams had a memorable sequence in which he had to take a chimpanzee for a walk: a bus conductor refuses to let them board his bus, causing Ken to protest with 'I've a good mind to report you to the RSPCA, cheeky monkey!' – which he follows by turning to the chimpanzee with an apologetic 'No offence!'

The main solo task of my character, Lily Duveen, is to collect the tickets at the door of a posh wine-tasting, and after she has finished her duty she is asked by the host whether she would like to join in the tasting:

–Are you a lover of the grape, Miss Duveen?
–No, actually, no – I never know what to do with the pips: you know, flick away, collect in the palm of the hand, or spit. Quite a social problem, don't you find?

Lily then samples the fare on offer so liberally that she cannot stand up (yet another falling-down role for Joan Sims). She gets roaring drunk, insults all and sundry, and is led away in disgrace.

On the day we were due to film the scene, I had first call on set, ready to shoot, at 8.30 a.m. When I reached the set our director Gerry Thomas said that everything was all in place, and we just needed a couple of quick run-throughs before shooting. We went through the scene a couple of times, and Gerry pronounced himself happy. Final make-up checks, everybody in place . . . action!

Things went according to plan until I took my first sip from a glass – and discovered to my horror that it contained neat gin: I'd been set up. I continued with the scene – my next line was 'Wow! That's what I really call a drink!' – until Gerry shouted, 'Right, we'll print that one – and I'll take Joanie off to sober her up!' That sort of jape was typical of the mood of the *Carry On* set even in the early days – very relaxed, very jokey, and always fun.

(One of the main actors in that scene was a very fresh-faced young man named Nicholas Parsons. Several years later, in 1967, I acted with Nick again in a farce named *Uproar in the House* at the Whitehall Theatre, during one performance of which his eccentric behaviour left me baffled. We were playing a love scene on the sofa at the back of the stage when, without saying a word to me, he suddenly got up and went down to the footlights, leaving me all alone and feeling very stupid: he

137

bent down, picked something up and tossed it into the orchestra pit, then came back and resumed his seat – and the dialogue. At the end of the play I asked him what the hell that had been all about, he'd broken up the scene completely – and he replied that he'd spotted a tiny scrap of paper lying on the stage and thought it might be distracting to the audience, so had got up to remove it. There's no answer to that.)

By now I had worked on four *Carry On*s in a row but was not able to appear in any of the next four – *Cruising*, *Cabby*, *Jack* or *Spying* – as I was heavily committed elsewhere, not only with comedy but also with the occasional serious role. In January 1961 BBC Television screened a play called *Off Centre*, in which the distinguished Canadian actor Cec Linder played the scientist Joe Hunter and I was his daughter-in-law named – guess! – Mavis. (A disproportionate percentage of the parts I've played over the years seem to have had the name Mavis or Madge.) But while serious drama was a challenge my heart was still in comedy, and of all the comedians with whom I worked at this period, few were as much fun to be with as Ted Ray. Whether on radio or television, Ted – who had in a previous life performed as Nedlo the Gypsy Violinist before settling for the more palatable name of Ted Ray – was simply one of the funniest men of his time, a brilliant comic who judged his timing to perfection. Working with him was always a hoot.

I particularly loved it when we were recording

his radio show up north. The whole cast and production team would commandeer a carriage for what was known as our 'train call'. The outward journey up to Manchester would be a fairly quiet affair, with actors soberly learning their lines and writers putting in late thoughts, but on the trip back to London we'd let our hair down, get out a few bottles and generally relax.

For a good while Ted's co-star in his show was Kitty Bluett, and after I'd replaced Kitty on the programme I was firmly put in my place on one of those northern trips. Ted and I were walking into the studio to do the recording when a fan loitering outside shouted at him: 'Oi, Ted, get Kitty back!' Charming . . .

Ted was a terrible tease, and since I at the time was an equally terrible prude, he used to make fun of me wickedly, pretending that I should drop my defences and have a fling with him. 'Go on,' he'd urge in mock supplication, 'get a bathing cap and take the plunge.' This was a sort of private catch-phrase between us – and so you may imagine my reaction when, during a quiet moment in the matinée of a show in which I was appearing in the West End, a voice from halfway back in the stalls suddenly shouted, 'Get a bathing cap!' I knew instantly who it was, and could scarcely contain my giggles for the rest of the scene.

Ted died in 1977, and I missed him dreadfully. My favourite story about him was of when he was King Rat in the Variety Club, the showbiz organisation which over the years has done so much good work and raised millions of pounds for worthy causes. At a big charity dinner Ted had been called upon to say grace, and he duly began in a soft voice:

'We thank you, Lord, for what we are about to receive . . .'

'Speak up!' came a pompous voice from the back of the room. 'We can't hear you!'

Ted replied: 'I'm not speaking to you.'

He was a great man.

At about this time my old friend from revue days Peter Myers got in touch. He was putting together a new revue with Ronnie Cass, John Pritchett and Alec Grahame, with additional material by Ray Galton and Alan Simpson, and wanted me in the line-up. I was thrilled to have the opportunity to work in revue again, and after a whistle-stop provincial tour which took in Newcastle, Liverpool, Leeds, Manchester and Brighton, *The Lord Chamberlain Regrets . . .!* opened in London at the Saville Theatre in June 1961.

A great team had been assembled. Fiz looked after the staging of the musical numbers, while sharing top billing with me were Ronnie Stevens, with whom I had worked so often in the early days, and Millicent Martin, a rapidly rising star of the musical stage who had been described as 'the female Danny Kaye' by the *New York Times* when appearing in *The Boy Friend* on Broadway.

The theatre programme (and the LP of the show which was issued during our London run) featured a large photograph of me resplendent in feather boa and tiara dripping with jewels, taken by none other than the great society photographer Norman Parkinson. I just loved my session at his studio. Tall, slim and wearing his famous little hat, he had an almost stately presence but was an exceedingly pleasant man to work with. He started off by asking me what my favourite music was, and when he learned that it was Frank Sinatra singing *Songs for Swinging Lovers* (what else?), put that on the record player to relax me while he clicked away.

Like other revues involving Peter Myers and Ronnie Cass, *The Lord Chamberlain Regrets . . . !* contained pieces with a cutting edge. The urge to make serious political points under the disguise of jolly musical comedy songs was particularly evident in 'The Ballad of Basher Green', written by Ronnie and Peter along with Dick Vosburgh and sung by Ronnie Stevens early in the second act:

I'll tell the tale
Of a husky male
Whose name was Basher Green.
He liked Joe Loss
And his brows grew right across
With nothing in between.
To get an idea beyond his ear
You would have to use dynamite.
He was dim at best and as you might have guessed
He was a Mosleyite.

This little ditty went on to describe how Basher

and his gang would patrol the streets around
Notting Hill Gate beating up black men:

> This is for the rights
> Of the decent whites
> I'm a fascist loyalist.

But Basher overdoes it when applying a bottled
sun-tan lotion, and his skin colour changes so
radically that next time he goes out he is mistaken
for a black man and set upon by his own gang,
who beat him up and leave him in the gutter.

> It was three whole days
> Before he could erase
> The effects of that bottled tan.
> By the time it was purged
> He had emerged
> A sadder but wiser man.
> He no longer traps frightened coloured chaps,
> 'Cos their skin's a thing they can't choose:
> That's how Basher Green learned what tolerance
>     can mean –
> Now he only beats up Jews.

Word of this song had got around among right-
wing groups from people who had seen the show
on its tour, and they did not like what they heard.
On the opening night at the Saville, as Ronnie
Stevens came to the end of the opening verse, a
group of Mosleyites in the audience suddenly
stood up and tried to howl him down. To his

142

eternal credit, he was not put off by this at all, and as Ronnie Cass at the piano continued to play over and over the bars introducing the next verse, Ronnie Stevens just announced 'I'll carry on when you're ready' and waited patiently for the disturbance to die down. After a few minutes' barracking the demonstrators were ejected by the theatre staff, and Ronnie resumed the song. It was a nasty incident, but it showed that satire could really strike a nerve.

Less controversial, though not much less satirical, was 'Business Arrangement', a sketch written by Eric Paice which I performed with Ronnie Stevens. This touched upon the British obsession with class, as seen through a conversation between a young girl and a young man who meet in a café and who are soon assessing the exact social category of themselves, their parents, and their friends George Rumble and Sandra Gibbons ('She thinks that by calling herself a receptionist that automatically makes her a business person – which of course it doesn't'). The girl comes to the point:

–You're not upper working, are you?
–It's very difficult to say what we are, actually. Economically we're upper working, yes, but socially we're definitely middle. People like George Rumble I'd suppose you'd say was sort of lower-upper-middle-working – except he's not working at the moment.
–That's just the same as Sandra. I'd call her lower

143

middle, though of course socially she is upper working, which is why I give her up, really.

Eventually the man gets round to asking the girl out, reasoning that 'seeing as how we're both business people, what say we call it a business arrangement?' But she rejects him with a crushing put-down:

–You know your trouble, don't you?
–What?
–You're common.

Whether in a sketch lampooning class prejudices, or in a fantasy about the *femme fatale* station announcer, the great thing about revue – at least as far as I was concerned – was that it made its point through making people laugh, and nothing in my live theatre career has given me a greater kick than the sound of laughter in response to my performance on stage. It comes back to this business of wanting to be wanted. My mother never actually told me that I was an unwanted child, but her story about the circumstances of her marriage to my father and how the other man had reappeared just too late was hardly calculated to make me feel I had been born into a home suffused with love. She used to tell other people how much she admired me, but she never told me, and the applause from a live audience in the theatre went a good way to filling that void.

For any comic actor, that interplay with the

audience is a priceless thing. You ride the laughs, or get through as quickly as you can if they're not responding; although it's not easy, you can usually coax them back if you've lost them. It's very much a two-way movement: they want you to make them laugh, you want them to laugh, but you have to achieve it together. And when you do, and when you can play your audience like an angler plays a fish – as I was usually able to do with 'Siren Song' – that's the best feeling in the world.

*Carry On* was not the only series of comedy films with which I was involved. The third *Doctor* film in which I acted – *Doctor in Love*, with Leslie Phillips – was released in 1960, and a few years later I appeared in my fourth, *Doctor in Clover* (again with Leslie): these were highly enjoyable to make, but never gave me the same buzz as the *Carry On*s in their prime.

Nor was there any shortage of cameo roles – in films like *No, My Darling Daughter*, which starred Michael Redgrave – and although these were not catapulting me to massive stardom, they were better than a slap in the belly with a wet fish. I had high hopes of *Mr Topaze*, directed by and starring Peter Sellers, but it was not very enthusiastically received and soon faded into obscurity. And there were plenty of *Carry On* connections in *Twice Round the Daffodils* – produced by Peter Rogers, directed by Gerry Thomas, written by Norman Hudis, with a cast which included Kenneth Williams. The glamour in the film came from Juliet

Mills, soon to join the *Carry On* team for *Carry On Jack*.

By now I was becoming something of an automatic choice for Peter Rogers and Gerald Thomas films, and I was delighted to be offered the female lead in *Nurse on Wheels*, a sort of *Carry On District Nurse*: I was even more pleased when I learned that the cast would include the great Athene Seyler, who had been such a help to me with *Breath of Spring*.

I'd started getting to grips with the script of *Nurse on Wheels* when there was a call from Peter Eade: they had decided to recast my role, and it was now to be played by Juliet Mills. I had been letting myself go a bit over the past couple of years, and the trim figure of Nurse Stella Dawson had been somewhat swamped by the effects of a few too many buns and gin and tonics: the blunt fact was that I was simply too round to play the glamorous female lead.

Peter Rogers was genuinely upset about removing me from the role, and offered me any other female part in the film; he even proposed a fee greater than I would have earned originally. I plumped (if you'll pardon the term) for the part of the daughter of the vicar.

That was a consolation prize, but the underlying problem would not go away so easily. I had been aware for a while that my weight was creeping up. I would put the pounds on very easily and very quickly, but getting them off was quite another matter. Now I decided that I had to do something

146

about it. So I started checking myself into Grayshott Hall, a wonderful health and fitness centre near Hindhead in Surrey and a haven to which I still return whenever I can. The regime of extremely healthy eating, no alcohol, plenty of relaxing massages and regular sessions in the swimming pool soon saw the weight coming off and my self-confidence coming back.

It wasn't easy, though, and one afternoon at Grayshott temptation overcame me. After a strict diet of lemon and water which had lasted two days, the inside of my mouth felt like the bottom of a parrot's cage and my spirits were low. I had been for a swim and was walking past the entrance to the 'light diet' lunch room when I happened to glance in. There, discarded on a plate waiting to be cleared away, was a single grape. I hung around in the corridor until there was nobody around, nipped in, grabbed the grape and hid it in my sponge bag – then rushed back to my room, put the 'Do Not Disturb' notice on the outside handle, turned the key in the lock, pulled the curtains and, trembling with excitement, removed my treasure from my sponge bag. I tucked into that grape like it was the last food I'd ever eat: the taste was sensational, but it didn't last long enough. Nor did each stay at Grayshott, but I invariably felt far less stressed, far fitter and far lighter on leaving than I had on arriving, and whenever I could afford it I'd make another retreat into the Surrey countryside.

\* \* \*

*Our House*, a television sitcom in which a group of people from very different backgrounds come together to live in one large house, was the brainchild of *Carry On* writer Norman Hudis and brought together several actors who were already staples of the *Carry On* gang. Hattie played Georgina Ruddy, a librarian who needed to make a great deal of noise at home to compensate for having to be quiet at work, Charlie Hawtrey, again the eccentric loner, worked in the council offices, and I was Daisy Burke, who moved from job to job on a regular basis.

Other television work including teaming up with three exceptional comic actors in Brian Rix (now Lord Rix), Dick Emery and Stanley Baxter, each of whom was full of laughs but also had those qualities which I have always admired above all others: one, sheer perfectionism, a refusal ever to settle for second best; two, discipline – for the unpredictable actor shows a disregard for his fellow actors which undermines the whole nature of the business; and three, the determination to stick out for what you really believe in. I like people who want to get down and graft rather than take the easy option and do only the minimum necessary.

I have Brian Rix to thank for forcing me – if only temporarily – to give up smoking. We were acting together in *Beside the Seaside*, a farce filmed on the stage of the Whitehall Theatre for transmission on television, and one of the scenes involved a passionate kiss between us. Clearly, kissing a smoker was not to Brian's liking – he was well known for his opposition to the weed, and had got most of his company to give up – so he tried to detach me from the habit by giving me all sorts of leaflets about the harm which smoking does. That didn't do the trick – I was firmly in the 'It'll never happen to me' camp – so he tried another tack: 'I hope you realise how unfeminine it is to smoke. You really smell. Your hair smells, your clothing smells, your breath is revolting – and I've got to go on stage and kiss you!'

This did sting. I went home, threw away my packet of cigarettes, washed my hair, put out clean clothes for the next day, and didn't smoke for six months. I only wish I'd kept it up.

Dick Emery and I got on like a house on fire, and my role as his female support on *The Dick Emery Show* on television was a barrel of laughs. Before I started working on the show I had been warned by others that he was such a perfectionist he could be hell to work with, but as it turned out nothing could have been further from the truth. Mind you, he did have his foibles. He hated having to look directly into the camera at the beginning of the show, and I used to distract him by going and standing behind the cameraman pulling silly faces at him.

Our director was John Street. Very tall and very slim with glistening white hair, he had two great terms of approbation: any action was either 'fain' or 'wandarful'. John's instructions used to crease Dick and myself up so much that we could not

149

look at each other while he was speaking to us, and I can still recall his lining us up for a scene in a Christmas special when I was playing the fairy on the Christmas tree: 'Now, Joan, I'm going to do this close-up on you, which will be wandarful, and I'm going to start with a long shot and track in and do a close-up on your wand, which will be fain, and Dick, you will approach Joan, which will be wandarful,' and so on.

Dick took a schoolboy delight in the subject of breaking wind, and since I was very much in the equivalent schoolgirls' camp he made a point of recording his own bouts of flatulence at home and playing a recording of them to me before the show. He'd lug his great big reel-to-reel tape recorder into the dressing room, plug it in and set it all up, then summon me. 'I've got some beauties for you today, Joan,' he'd promise – and then we'd both sit there screeching with laughter as the recorder did its bit.

I sometimes thought that there wasn't a great deal of difference between the off-screen Dick and the on-screen. If we went out for lunch he'd take great delight in setting off down the street with the little mincing walk of his 'Ooh, you are awful – but I like you!' lady (who, incidentally, was very strongly based on a real person in the production team). He'd also delight in buying me daft presents – like the time he nipped into a chemist's shop, saying, 'I'm just going to get you something,' and a few moments later emerged holding a horrible plastic container, done up with a rose on top to look like some sort of presentation box, filled to the brim with old hair rollers. He certainly knew the way to a girl's heart . . .

Stanley Baxter and I had first worked together in *The Happy Ha'penny* at the Glasgow Citizens' Theatre all those years ago, and I had been an admirer of his ever since, so it was a joy to be with him again. We were rehearsing *The Stanley Baxter Show* in a rehearsal room just off the Edgware Road, and having broken for lunch Stanley and I were scouring the area for somewhere to eat. It looked like the best bet for a decent meal was the fish and chip shop, the front of which proudly proclaimed the establishment to be a member of the Federation of Fish Mongers. That sounded a pretty good recommendation, so Stanley and I went in for cod and chips and all the trimmings. We were tucking in when I realised that the two people behind the counter – the woman who dispensed the fish and the man who shovelled on the chips – were whispering to each other, nudging and pointing over at us. Eventually the woman could contain herself no longer. She approached our table.

'Excuse me – but it's Shirley Malane, isn't it?'

I pulled myself up to my full height and put on a show of mock indignation: 'Don't you mean Shirley Maclaine?'

'Yes, that's right!'

'No, sorry – I'm not.'

'And I suppose she thinks I'm Rock Hudson,' whispered Stanley in my ear.

Just what Shirley Maclaine might have been doing scoffing her lunch in a chippy on the Edgware Road does not seem to have occurred to the poor lady, but in any case she retreated in confusion. Stanley and I were too hysterical to be able to return to our lunch, so we left the fish and chips congealing on the plates and made a hasty exit.

By that time, with the *Carry On* series becoming increasingly popular and my face getting familiar on television, being accosted or stared at was simply an occupational hazard, and though I'd sometimes wear dark glasses to avoid being recognised, I realised that it was all part of the life. In any case, dark glasses did nothing to disguise my voice, and it was the sound of that as much as my appearance which got heads turning.

One day I was walking up the street minding my own business when I was suddenly grabbed from behind and pinned against the wall. No, it wasn't a mugger; it was an elderly lady, who screamed down the street at her friend: ''Ere, Elsie! Look what I've got!'

Thus summoned, Elsie came hurrying up, and when she saw who it was, shoved her face right up to mine and demanded:

'That Sid James – what's he really like?'

'He's – er – he's very nice,' was about all I could stammer, and, disappointed, they trudged off.

But there can be a much darker side to having a well-known face.

When I was living with Tony Baird in the Wilton

Place flat, I was told by Peter Eade's office that a lady was very keen to come and see me. Her young sister, a great fan of mine, was gravely ill in hospital with leukaemia, and seeing me in a *Carry On* role was the only thing that had made the poor girl laugh for months: the elder sister wanted to bring round a box of chocolates to thank me. I couldn't see much harm in that, so suggested that she be given my address and asked to come on a day when I would be at the flat, working my way through the fan mail with Peter's assistant Laurena. I did think that if a stranger was going to come into the house, there had better be someone else present. Still, when Mary Hennessy – as she called herself – arrived at the front door there was nothing to suggest that she could pose any sort of threat. She was Irish, neat and quietly spoken, and very polite when asked to come up. Declining a drink of any sort, she sat down in the sitting room and started chattering away, though some of what she was saying seemed a little odd. 'I've no interest in film stars myself,' she declared, but carried on gabbling and made no attempt to leave. My suspicions were aroused more when I asked if she'd like a signed photograph for her sister. 'Yes . . . thanks,' she replied hesitantly, as if she had forgotten about her sister completely, 'that would be fine, that would be fine.' At this moment Laurena was out of the room, but since Mary Hennessy was obviously no threat to me I slipped out to fetch the photo. When I came back and gave it to her, she took it without looking at it, and made to leave when I suggested that I had work to do and must get on.

'Of course, of course,' she said. 'You will come and see my sister in hospital, won't you?'

I asked which hospital her sister was in, but she avoided the question and departed.

Within a couple of days I realised that while I had been out of the room fetching the photograph she had nipped across to the phone and made a note of my number. Her first few calls were on the same subject: when was I going to visit her sister? Still she wouldn't tell me where this sister was, so I avoided saying I'd go and visit her. As Mary became more frustrated, so her calls became more threatening, and by now I was getting really worried about what she might do next.

On the opposite corner from the flat was the local post office, outside which stood two telephone boxes, and one day I was looking out of the window across the street just as the phone rang. I glanced across to the phone box, and sure enough, there was Mary Hennessy. She was making the calls from across the street! 'Come to the front door,' she said, 'I've something to show you' – but I declined. The following day brought another call – more frustrated, more abusive: 'If you don't go and see my sister in hospital and she dies, that will be on your conscience for the rest of your life.' The next call turned the screw tighter: 'Do you think I'm going to stick a knife in your back? Are you that scared of me? If you don't believe my story, go and ask at St Mary Abbot's Hospital, where I work as a nurse: they'll tell you all about me.'

Tony, who was as alarmed by all this as I was, went to that hospital and made enquiries. Mary Hennessy had indeed been a nurse there, but had left after suffering a mental illness. She did have a sister, but as far as they knew at the hospital she was perfectly fit and healthy.

We realised then that we were dealing with someone who was mentally disturbed, but what could we do? The police were sympathetic but could take no action unless and until she actually attacked me.

This went on for about six months, the tension being gradually cranked up as I wondered what Mary was going to say – or do – next. She started calling in the middle of the night, and on one occasion said that if I didn't go downstairs straight away and open the door to her she'd get in her car, drive up the motorway and crash, and it would be all my fault and on my conscience for ever.

The following day Tony and I were having a drink in the flat with our neighbours Bill and Holl, discussing what I should do, when the buzzer went. I knew it would be her, and asked Tony to go down and talk to her. He came back a few minutes later to report that Mary Hennessy had been standing at the front door with a large man's handkerchief tied round her head like a bandana, and smudges of lipstick all down her face. She had asked:

'Is Miss Sims in?'

'No, but I'm her boyfriend. Can I give her a message?'

'No, no, it's all right' – and with that she turned and scurried up the road.

She rang the next morning.

'Joan, it's Mary. I thought I'd better ring and tell you my sister died in the night.'

'Well, Mary,' I replied, 'considering how very ill she was, it's probably a blessing for her that she's gone.'

I never heard from Mary Hennessy again. Her little fantasy was over.


That had been a horrible experience, the unwelcome side of my having become a fairly well-known personality in film and on television. But there was of course a much brighter side – notably a significant improvement in the bank balance.

I had long harboured the dream of having my own house, and in 1963 – through Bernard Walsh, a very old friend and an estate agent – I bought a lovely Victorian terraced house in Hurlingham Road, Fulham. After the confined space of a succession of flats, this was like being out on the prairie: it had five levels, and looked out across the road on to a large playground. That open location was something of a mixed blessing, however, since the playground offered a fine view of the house to anyone planning a little uninvited visit, and I was burgled three times – once by a fourteen-year-old boy who turned out to have eighty-seven previous convictions! On another occasion I came downstairs to find a lad of about sixteen standing in the kitchen. When I asked him, ever so calmly, what he was doing there, he said he wanted to know the way to Parsons Green tube station. Although I was sweating buckets – after all, he could have had a knife – I managed to control myself: 'Young man, I think you know where Parsons Green tube station is, and I suggest you go there – and if you don't do so quickly I'll call my husband down.' He went meekly out the front door.

Less directly threatening but a more regular nuisance was the succession of people who were just curious to know where a well-known face lived. I was hardly Elizabeth Taylor, but it was almost a daily occurrence to hear the letterbox banging as some juvenile peered through looking for a glimpse of the famous Joan Sims, and I'd hear these snatches of conversation:

'This is where she lives!'
'Can you see her?'
'No . . .'

Hurlingham Road looked genteel enough, but that did not prevent muggings taking place out there, and my car was broken into or damaged several times. Much more tragic was the case of the confused and arthritic old lady who lived next door to me. One day she came in and insisted that she leave me £10: 'This is in case I need to get away.' The next morning when I got up I looked out the back and saw two policemen peering through her window. It turned out that she had taken an overdose.

Such a catalogue of misfortune makes Hurlingham Road sound a pretty blighted place to live, but for most of the time I revelled in the space my house gave me – and it can't have been too bad, as I lived in it for sixteen years.

One of my near neighbours was Ted Dicks, a very good friend and brilliant musical collaborator with my old mate Myles Rudge; my part as Mavis Willis in the radio comedy series *Something to Shout About* brought me into contact with Myles again, and it was through him and Ted that in 1963 I made my brief foray into the world of pop music.

During the early 1960s there had grown up a vogue for novelty songs recorded by comic actors. Perhaps the best-known examples were the two songs with which Bernard Cribbins – who appeared in *Carry On Jack* and *Carry On Spying* (neither of which I was in myself) – stormed the pop charts in 1962: 'Hole in the Ground' and 'Right Said Fred' both made the Top Ten, and both were written by Myles and Ted, who suggested to me that with all my experience in revue I was an obvious candidate to record a silly song or two. I was persuaded, and after a few rehearsals around the piano turned up for my recording session with the Johnnie Spence Orchestra. Our producer was none other than George Martin, not yet the legend of his business which he was very soon to become, but an exceptionally easy and kindly man to work with.

The 'A' side was 'Oh Not Again Ken', the impassioned plea of a girl in the back row to her boyfriend to stop molesting her and concentrate on the film:

> Oh not again Ken,
> I'll tell you when, Ken,
> Wait until the picture begins to start.
> Through the news and trailer you was blowin'
>     in me ear;
> Me Mum would die if she was 'ere,
> So oh not again Ken,
> Honestly men, Ken,
> S'pose the lady usherette turns and sees:
> It's not nice, Ken,
> Told you twice, Ken,
> So not again Ken please . . .
>
> Oh not again Ken,
> Count up to ten, Ken,
> Get yourself a choc-ice and do cool down.
> Never knew a fella who created such a fuss:
> Like sitting next to an octopus,
> So oh not again, Ken,
> Maybe now and then, Ken,
> But you're forever taking liberties.
> You're no gent, Ken,
> Me earring's getting bent, Ken,
> Oh not again Ken, please.

The 'B' side to this steamy account of 'larky goings-on in the two-and-threes' was another cry from the heart entitled 'Hurry Up Gran', with the girl begging her elderly grandmother to get a move on with her ablutions as the rest of the family was queuing up to use the bathroom:

Hurry up Gran, get a move on, do:
You've got no right on a Saturday night
To be in there scrubbing for an hour or more –
I'm here knocking on the bathroom door.
You oughta hurry up Gran, there's a great long queue,
Poor Aunt Kate's in a terrible state
'Cos she heard you singing and you sounded like a man.
('Go away, Mavis!')
Hurry up, Gran!

With that famed versatility, I both sang Mavis's annoyance and spoke Gran's indignant replies (such as 'I'm practising me breast-stroke . . .').

This disc didn't cut much ice in the charts, but I got to mime to it a few times on television shows (never quite reaching the giddy heights of *Top of the Pops*). I saw the record as another string to my bow rather than any serious attempt to break into the pop world, and leapt at the chance of issuing a follow-up. In 'Spring Song' I'm sitting on an ancient sofa holding hands with the same boyfriend ('Oh Ken, I shouldn't really, but I can't resist you when you waggle your ears like that'), and the furniture starts to show its age:

160

Oh that spring, it isn't very nice
Since we've been here talking I've been
   vaccinated twice
Can't you fix it with a piece of string?
Whenever I'm near you
DOINNGG! goes the spring.

The flipside, 'Men', was rather less of a novelty song than the earlier efforts, more the universal expression of exasperation by a girl thoroughly fed up with the way she's being treated by the opposite sex:

We've got this special date
And he's half an hour late
But that's men.
He sorta lets it fall
I should be glad he's there at all
But that's men.
Concerning where we'll go
He lets me know
The casting vote is his;
If there's some film that I think nice,
He's been and seen it twice
Already . . .

Again the record made little impact, and in any case our producer George Martin's attention was by now being distracted by a promising new pop group – three guitar players and a drummer – that a man called Brian Epstein had discovered in a club in Liverpool.

After my break with Tony Baird my mother had never actually said, 'I told you so,' but once he had departed from my life it proved possible to build bridges with my parents. The rift had caused deep wounds on both sides and it took a good while for anything like my old relationship with my mother and father to be restored. But I went down to Southchurch to see them as often as I could, and on the whole found them in good shape.

Then I heard that my father had had a bout of bronchitis and had been admitted to hospital. At first this did not sound too serious, but one day while I was recording *The Dick Emery Show* I received word that he had taken a turn for the worse and I should get down to see him. Peter Eade, as always showing friendship and concern way beyond the call of an agent's duty, drove me to Essex and straight to the hospital. My father was clearly in a bad way – very weak, and his fingers had gone blue – and I could understand, up to a point, why my mother had not felt able to come and see him. I sat with him for a while, and as I was about to leave I bent down to kiss him, at which moment he looked me straight in the eye before whispering: 'You will look after your mother, won't you?' He died that night – and, though we were not told this until after he had gone, the cause of his death turned out to be not bronchitis, but incurable cancer of the lungs and stomach.

My mother did not come to the crematorium for

the funeral service. She simply could not face it, and stayed behind at the house to prepare the food for when the mourners returned.

The death of my father left a terrible void for both my mother and myself, and although this was a very traumatic time for me, for my mother the transition was understandably much more difficult. Daddy had done everything regarding the running of the household – he was always fastidious about going to the electricity and gas offices to pay the bills, for example – and now she had to cope for herself. Admirably, she adopted a very positive attitude, throwing herself into fresh activities. There was a lovely old lady we knew called Dolly Brockman who lived on the coast and was crippled with arthritis, and my mother would go and help her out. She even started pottery classes, and gradually settled into a busy life on her own.

For me, it was a case of knuckling down and getting on with my acting career.

In July 1964 I rejoined the *Carry On* gang at Pinewood for one of the very best of the series, *Carry On Cleo* – written, like every *Carry On* since *Cabby*, by Talbot Rothwell. As Calpurnia, the wife of Julius Caesar (Kenneth Williams), I was able to indulge my love of dressing up, and for once the costumes were made for me, rather than my having to resort to some old dress that had been used before and had to have a new panel sewn in the back to accommodate my girth – which by now was unvaryingly plump. Echoing the scenes of Amanda Barrie as Cleopatra bathing in asses' milk, Calpurnia's first appearance finds her in the bath awaiting the return of Caesar, who has been off conquering foreign lands, and soon establishes her as the shrewish wife: 'Where've you been for the last three years?' she yells at him as he enters.

The sets of *Carry On Cleo* were a sizeable cut above what we usually had for the series, as shooting of *the* film of *Cleopatra*, with Elizabeth Taylor and Richard Burton, had recently been halted at Pinewood and moved on – leaving the studio with these lavish Egyptian sets, which we hastened to commandeer. Sheer luxury.

Away from the *Carry On*s, there were plenty of other film roles at this time, including *The Big Job* with Sid James, Dick Emery, Sylvia Syms, Lance Percival and Jim Dale. In that film I played the predatory widowed landlady determined to get her claws into Dick Emery, and it was starting to dawn on me that I was being called upon rather too much to play shrill, overbearing middle-aged ladies. Sometimes I yearned for something a little more subtle.

*San Ferry Ann*, a silent comedy about a British family going on holiday in France, took me to the fabulously glamorous location of Calais, where I shared a room with Barbara Windsor. One day while we were in our room waiting for the call, Barbara lay on the bed busily writing postcards.

'How can you muster any enthusiasm for sending postcards from this awful place?' I asked her.

'You know what my family's like. They think when I'm abroad it's posh. They don't know Calais's a shit-hole, do they?'

She'd summed it up so well, but then, Barbara was always one for speaking her mind. One evening on that same trip I was walking across the hotel restaurant to join the rest of the team for dinner, and when I arrived at the table Barbara exclaimed: ''Ere, Joanie – I don't know why they don't let you play more sexy roles. You've got triffic legs!'

Dear Barbara – I do take my hat off to her. She's made a fantastic job of reinventing herself through her own guts and determination – I never worked with a tougher cookie than Babs – and joining *EastEnders* as Peggy not only gave her career a new lease of life, but showed to the world the serious actress lurking all along inside that fluffy *Carry On* personality.

If 'Oh Not Again Ken' and its follow-up had shown me that my destiny was not to be a pop star, I still got a terrific buzz from musical theatre, and in the summer of 1964 leapt at the chance to play in a new musical which we tried out in Kilburn before moving to the Piccadilly Theatre in the West End. This was *Instant Marriage*, written by Bob Grant with music by Laurie Holloway. The plot concerned all sorts of convolutions involving Lavinia, an innocent girl from the north (me) coming south, getting involved with a marriage bureau and inadvertently becoming a stripper, but my main memory of the show is the sheer joy of singing in a musical – and especially that magical feeling which, whatever the show, I experienced at the first band call. It's all very well singing to a rehearsal piano, but the first time with the full orchestra always made the hairs on the back of my neck stand up.

I had some great numbers in *Instant Marriage*, but my favourite song was one that involved asking the telegraph service what it would cost to send a message to the marriage bureau, composed – in order to keep the cost down – in that strange truncated language of telegrams:

I come eight, I excited, I not sleep;
I can't wait, I so happy, I could weep;
Much bewildered, in flat spin, but look forward
    to begin,
I come eight, I excited, I not sleep.

I much smile, I delighted, I meet him;
Little while, cup of happiness will brim;
Got new costume, likewise hat, got all trousseau,
    bring all that;
I come eight, I excited, I not sleep.

At a party during the run of *Instant Marriage* my estate agent friend Bernard Walsh introduced me to a gorgeous black-haired hunk from Yorkshire with a twinkling eye and wicked sense of humour. I knew nothing about cricket, but even I had heard of the great bowler Fred Trueman, and

166

meeting him in the flesh was quite something. Fred and I hit it off immediately, and he insisted that he wanted to come and see the show. Not only was he as good as his word, he brought with him what appeared to be the entire England cricket team. Afterwards Fred came backstage with a huge bouquet of flowers for me – what a gent! I wish I could say that I repaid the compliment by going to watch an England cricket game, but I never did.

Perhaps because of the inaccessibility of the Piccadilly Theatre – which I always thought was too tucked away to attract really big audiences – *Instant Marriage* did not last as long as it should have. But I loved it.

In July 1965 we started filming *Carry On Cowboy*, which has remained one of my all-time favourites. For a start, there were the costumes. By then I hated wearing uniforms (as in *Constable*) but adored the sort of lavish dresses that I was able to wear in *Cowboy*. I also relished the whole atmosphere of the set – the men loved every minute of dressing up as cowboys and playing with their guns – and in Jim Dale, better known as a singer and disc jockey and now in his first *Carry On* role, I was sure I was witnessing a real star of the future. Jim had a wonderfully easy-going personality and straight away fitted into the spirit of the *Carry Ons*. He was also amazingly athletic, and had no hesitation about performing his own stunts (most famously on the runaway hospital trolley in *Carry On Doctor*).

Tolly Rothwell's script for *Carry On Cowboy* gave me one of the best entrances of my whole film career.

Sid James – The Rumpo Kid – is standing at the bar drinking a shot of whisky when the glass is shattered in his hand by a bullet fired by the voluptuous lady slinking her way down the stairs. She goes up to the bar and confronts him.

–I'll just take that gun of yours, cowboy.
–What for?
–I don't allow no shooting at my place.
–Lady, I wouldn't dream of shooting at your place.

She indicates her own gun – 'I'm not afraid to use this, you know' – and he hands his own weapon over. She's impressed:

–My, but you've got a big one.
–I'm from Texas, ma'am – we've all got big ones down there.

The Rumpo Kid then discovers that she is Belle, owner of the saloon.

–So you're Belle.
–Yeah. My intimate friends call me Ding Dong.
–I'd like to give you a clang some time.

Someone told me that the review of *Cowboy* in the *Daily Telegraph* described me as 'a majestically awesome saloon queen'. I've been called a few things in my time, but 'majestically awesome' was a first.

Less than six months after we'd finished filming *Cowboy* we were at Pinewood again for *Carry On Screaming!*, in which, as Emily Bung, wife of Detective Sergeant Sidney Bung (played by Harry H. Corbett), I was back in my customary role of shrewish wife. One strand of the plot – despite what you may remember, *Carry On* films *do* have plots – concerned the business of Doctor Watt (Kenneth Williams) abducting young women, immersing them in a huge vat of wax and transforming them into shop dummies, and when it was time for poor Emily Bung to become the next victim, I had to have a plaster cast taken of my entire body.

I was dispatched to the studio plasterers' shop, where I had to strip down to my underwear and lie on a table. I was then coated in plaster of Paris, one section of my body at a time, with lengths of string laid in strategic places to create a seam so that the cast could be easily removed once the plaster had dried. It was then the turn of my head to be caked in plaster, with a drinking straw stuck up each nostril to allow me to breathe. The whole process took about an hour. Oh, the things I had to do for my art!

*Screaming!* was my seventh *Carry On*, and since the films were now receiving extensive exposure overseas, almost unwittingly I was becoming well known in far-flung corners of the globe. Even so, it was something of a surprise to be called quite out of the blue early in 1966 by John Troke, who was responsible for publicising the *Carry On*s, and asked if I fancied a trip to South America to appear in a film festival at a place called Cartagena, near Bogotá in Colombia.

Among the movies being featured at the festival was *Billy Liar*, and the original idea was for the British film industry to be represented by the two stars of that film, Julie Christie and Tom Courtenay. For some reason Julie had to withdraw, and I was invited to be her substitute, as British comedy films – including the *Carry On*s – were very popular in Colombia. Then it turned out that Tom could not go either, and for a while the whole trip seemed to be in jeopardy. After a few days of worry I got a call from John Troke. It was definitely going ahead: Colombia here we come!

I was just recovering from a dose of glandular fever, so the prospect of a trip to somewhere new, exciting and hot was a godsend, and I immediately started making plans. The first thing I did was to phone one of the costume designers who worked on the *Carry On* films at Pinewood: I was going to South America – what should I wear? She was wonderfully helpful, going so far as to accompany me around the shops while I bought all the necessary gear to make the transition from a cold English climate to the warmth of the southern hemisphere.

The flight was not quite as the crow flies – I seem to remember going via Paris and Madrid –

but after what felt like an eternity in transit (soothed by plenty of champagne along the way) John and I arrived in Bogotá, where we were met by Malcolm Billington, who was organising the British representation at the film festival, and taken to Cartagena.

My first job on arrival was to address all those attending the festival from the stage of a theatre which felt about as big as the Palladium. But there was a hitch. I spoke no Spanish whatsoever. What was I to do? Malcolm Billington reassured me:

'Just go on the stage and say, "Viva Cartagena!"'

'Will that be enough?'

'They'll love it – you'll see!'

And so I smoothed down my little white dress, went up on the stage, stood in front of the microphone and amid a great babble of shouting announced:

'Viva Cartagena!'

There was a bedlam of applause – I'd never got such a rapturous response for such a brief performance – and that about wound up my official duties.

The following morning the local press was full of the appearance of 'The Little White One'. All of a sudden I was a celebrity, and I loved it. The papers carried stories about a person variously described as *la actriz comica* or *brillante artista del cinema ingles* or *las simpatica rubia inglesa* who *rie mucho y mucho hace reir* (the last bit means, I'm reliably assured, 'who laughs a lot and makes others laugh a lot'). One paper described me as *la señorita Sims, cuaranta anos, soltera, sin novio y hartas ganas de casarse* – 'Miss Sims, forty years old [cheek! I was thirty-five], unmarried, without a lover and "desperately anxious to get married"'.

The film festival lasted just one week, at the end of which John Troke returned to England. But I was having such a whale of a time that I decided to stay – and I'm glad I did. I was treated like royalty – given the freedom of the city of Cartagena, taken out to play with the local kids, and, having been provided with the services of a wonderful interpreter named Josephina, shown round all the local sights. There was even a running of the bulls staged especially in my honour – though I have to say that I was on the side of the bulls.

Then there were the parties: parties in people's houses, parties at the Hotel Americano, the oceanside hotel where I was staying, and – best of all – parties on the beach. Just imagine: here was the little girl from the station house at Laindon sipping rum and Coca-Cola and dancing the night away under the Colombian moon, while the waves crashed against the shore. Sheer magic. After one beach party I retired exhausted to my room, only to be awakened at four in the morning by the steel band striking up outside my bedroom door: they had been sent by an admirer to serenade me!

I'd never had a better time in my life, but it was too good to last, and I was brought back to earth one morning with a telegram from Peter Eade: 'PUT DOWN OR STOP WHATEVER YOU ARE

DOING AND COME HOME AND EARN SOME MONEY.' He was right: I'd been in South America five weeks instead of the one week originally planned, and I had to go back.

When I went to check out from the Hotel Americano, the manager presented me with an envelope. In it was a card explaining that, while it was customary for stars to give autographs to their admirers, Joan Sims had been such an exemplary guest of the hotel that she was being awarded a special certificate:

CERTIFICO, que la Señorita Joan Sims, artista de merecida fama, es una persona de encantador caracter, simpatica y de un trato, con los que han tenido la suerte de frecuentarlo, magnifico. Como consideramos que estas cualidades son extra-ordinariamente raras entre los miembros de su profession es que extendemos al presente.

You can't say fairer than that.

# 6

# Carrying On . . .

In September 1966 I was back at Pinewood to start filming *Carry On – Don't Lose Your Head*.

This was the thirteenth *Carry On* film – my eighth – and by now the series was in full swing, hugely popular with the cinema-going public and no less so with the actors and crew. Gathering at the studios for each new picture was like going back to school after the holidays – meeting old chums and sharing all the jokes and gossip. We knew that we had a few weeks of fun ahead of us.

*Don't Lose Your Head*, a characteristic *Carry On* romp through the French Revolution, was one of my very favourites. It was certainly one of the funniest of all the *Carry On*s, and as Desirée Dubarry, sidekick of Kenneth Williams's Citizen Camembert, I could indulge my love of acting in period costume. Some of Tolly Rothwell's dialogue was extremely clever, and I particularly liked the exchange between Kenny, Peter Butterworth (Citizen Bidet) and myself when, posing as aristocrats, we arrive at a country mansion after an arduous journey in a horse-drawn carriage. Camembert helps a grimacing Desirée Dubarry out of the carriage:

*Camembert:* Come along – what's the matter with you?

*Dubarry:* It's all these hump-back bridges and these English roads. I shan't be able to sit down for a week.

*Camembert:* I do wish you wouldn't be so vulgar. Kindly remember you're supposed to be an aristocrat.

*Dubarry:* Don't they have bottoms then?

*Camembert:* Of course they do, but they don't refer to them as such. Down here they're called country seats.

*Dubarry:* What do they call them in London?

*Camembert:* Surely you've heard of the London *derrière*?

*Dubarry:* Well, it'll be a long time before I can put my *derrière* on a country seat.

At this time life was treating me pretty well. I was very busy, with television and the stage as well as films, I had my house in Hurlingham Road, and if it wasn't exactly a matter of being catapulted to fame and fortune, I was better off than I had ever been. So I decided it was time for a treat – and what would suit my mood better than a brand new car? I'd learnt to drive while living in Wilton Place, and having a little Mini in which I could nip around London gave me a freedom I'd previously lacked. Now it was time for something a little more trendy.

I went down to Dove's showroom in Streatham, picked out a lovely little white Triumph Herald convertible – very much the 'in' car of the time – and ordered one to be picked up later in the week.

The next day we were continuing to shoot *Don't Lose Your Head*. The first person I met at Pinewood was Norah Holland, who since first coming to act as my stand-in early in the *Carry On* series had become one of my best friends. 'I've just ordered a new car!' I told her gleefully, but when she heard what I was paying for it she was amazed.

'You mean you're paying the full price?'

'Of course.'

'But no one pays the full price for a car. You always haggle over a discount.'

This was news to poor innocent Joanie, who thought that if something had a price on it, that was what you paid, and the gloss was beginning to wear off the bright mood which my new purchase had put me in.

Half an hour later I was being made up, and in came Sid James, who off-screen was just as much a wheeler-dealer when it came to money as many of the characters he played. I could guess what was coming.

'I hear you've bought a brand new car, Joan – and that you paid full price for it! No one pays full price for a car.'

Muttering my appreciation of this observation, I

went on to the set, where the first thing that Gerald Thomas said to me was: 'Joan, what's all this about you paying full price for a new car?'

I could have screamed, but managed just to say to Gerald that I simply wasn't aware of all the ins and outs of buying cars, and I was very upset to be told by everyone in sight that I'd been so naïve.

'Don't you worry,' he said, 'leave it to your Uncle Gerald' – and by the end of that day he had been in touch with Geoffrey Dove himself, chairman of the company from which I was buying the car (who, as luck would have it, turned out to be a friend of his) and had negotiated me a good discount – in return for a few publicity photographs showing 'Miss Joan Sims enjoying the comfort of her new Triumph Herald from Dove's'. It was a typical piece of helpfulness by Gerald.

The following week I was driving down to Pinewood minding my own business when I was involved in a minor collision with another car. As I slowed down on the approach to the Hogarth Roundabout, one of the busiest junctions in West London, the car behind bumped into me. I was horrified – not only by the prang, but also by the sudden realisation that while I knew there were certain things a driver had to do if there was an accident, I had no idea what they were. But I was determined not to lose face and let the other driver think he'd got away with it. After we'd both pulled over I got out of my car. Affecting an air of great determination, I went round and examined the front (a highly intelligent move, considering that it was the back that had been run into), then went to the rear – no significant damage there – and then had the brainwave of going round the car kicking each of the tyres.

What a strange sight it must have made to other drivers in the rush-hour traffic swirling round the Hogarth Roundabout – the driver of the other car standing there saying nothing, just staring at this dotty woman going round her car kicking the tyres ... Eventually I finished kicking, and told the other driver, 'I don't think you've done any damage' – at which point, still not having uttered a word, he got back into his car and drove off.

I was in quite an agitated state by the time I arrived at the studio and told Norah what had happened. As she helped me clamber into my costume for my first scene in *Don't Lose Your Head* that morning – a tightly corseted gown with a hooped petticoat – she launched into a list of what I should have done and generally sent me up for being such a dimwit.

As luck would have it, Eric Morecambe and Ernie Wise were filming at Pinewood that day, and when word reached them about my little accident they couldn't resist the chance for a bit of impromptu comedy. They strode into my dressing room. 'Have you heard about this maniac who's had a prang?' was Eric's opening line, and then they launched into this amazing routine, with Eric making out he'd been driving down the A4 towards the Hogarth Roundabout that morning and nudged the car in front – the driver of which turned out to be a real Dizzy Lizzy who got out and went round kicking her tyres . . .

Within a few seconds I was hysterical with laughter.

'Eric, stop, stop!' But Eric Morecambe in full comic flight was not easily reined in. By the time he'd finished there was only one place I had to go.

'Norah, you're going to have to help me!' – and I lifted up my hooped skirts above my head (thus completely blinding myself) while Norah guided me along the corridor and through the loo door. She then had to pull down my knickers and sit me on the seat while I did the necessary. When I'd finished she pulled up my knickers and, with me still holding the hooped skirts over my head, guided me back to the dressing room.

'I don't know,' said Norah as we sat down, exhausted by this manoeuvre: 'I've been a stand-in, I've been a double, I've been a stunt driver – but I've never been called upon to pull down an artist's knickers so that she can have a wee.'

The next *Carry On* film was *Follow That Camel*. The lead role of Sergeant Nocker was originally intended for Sid James, but poor Sid was laid low with a heart condition, and, under pressure from the distributors Rank to increase the international appeal of the series and thus boost income overseas, Peter Rogers brought in Phil Silvers, star of the wonderful *Bilko* series which seemed to have been running on television for ever.

I had a very small part in the voluptuous shape of Zig-Zig, described by one reviewer as the 'eye-flashing, bosom-wobbling owner of the local low dive'. For once I was released from the confines of buxom blonde roles and fitted with a wig of cascading jet-black hair to become . . . a buxom brunette. The desert scenes were shot at Camber Sands in Sussex, but Zig-Zig herself never got further than the back lot at Pinewood; missing out on all the camaraderie of travelling to the locations made me feel a bit left out, and not quite as much a part of the team as I usually was.

Kenneth Williams got increasingly irritated with Phil Silvers, partly because he claimed to find him boring (but then Kenny found lots of people boring) and partly because of professional irritation at the imported American star's having to use 'idiot boards' – large boards on which your words are written up and from which you can read if you are not sure of your lines. Certainly Phil Silvers had no recourse to idiot boards during any of my scenes with him, and I found him charming personally and completely on the ball professionally: perhaps Kenny just didn't like being upstaged by a big star.

Never mind Kenny's quibbling: my own encounter with Phil Silvers provided one of my all-time favourite *Carry On* lines, when after giving him a ride on my donkey I turn to take my leave of him with the words: 'I have a good ass, no?'

Although I was now an established member of the *Carry On* team, there was also plenty of work coming in for television and radio.

For my part as Gran in the legendary BBC television sitcom *Till Death Us Do Part* the stock Giles-cartoon Grandma character which I'd been using since my am-dram days in Laindon really came into its own, as did my similarly lifelong ability to make myself look as if I had no teeth. Playing Gran meant exercising extreme self-control, as if I corpsed – that is, broke out laughing rather than keeping in character – I'd reveal my teeth, and it was essential to remain toothless throughout.

The cast was wonderful – notably, of course, Warren Mitchell as Alf Garnett and Dandy Nichols as his 'silly old moo' wife Else – but the true glory of this series was the writing. Johnny Speight's scripts were quite superb, and for me the fascinating thing about them was that paraphrasing his words simply would not work. Each part was so tightly written that it had to be learned and delivered word for word, otherwise the rhythm would be lost.

In one episode I had a speech which went on for a whole page of script, and I was having such great difficulty learning it that I confided in our producer Dennis Main Wilson: like that dreaded phrase 'petty falsehood' way back in *Breath of Spring*, this speech was an obstacle in my way, and the knowledge that I had to face it was making me so nervous that I could not play the scene properly. Dennis suggested that I have an idiot board just off camera, but Warren insisted that this was not the answer: 'Joan, if you rely on an idiot board it'll be the beginning of the end. It doesn't matter a damn if we have to retake the scene ten times. If you use that board your spontaneity will be destroyed.' He was so right, and he saved me from starting down the slippery slope: I learned the speech, and had no further problem.

The sitcom *Sam and Janet*, which started on ITV in June 1967 after a good run on radio, was the story of the Marshalls (I was Janet and John Junkin was Sam – though David Kossoff had played the part on radio), a suburban married couple in middle age – a sort of precursor of *Terry and June*. After twenty episodes on the radio and six on the television I thought that was enough of Janet for me, and Vivienne Martin took the part for the second series, screened early in 1968.

*Seven Year Hitch* was a one-off sitcom for the BBC's series *Comedy Playhouse* in which I starred with my old chum Harry H. Corbett: Harry was Ern, boss of a failing dance school, and I played his wife Isabel, known as 'Is'. Harry's previous appearance in *Comedy Playhouse* was in the pilot that became *Steptoe and Son*, but *Seven Year Hitch* never made it to a series.

Amid all this broadcast comedy, revue had not been completely forgotten. *Before the Fringe* was an attempt by television to display some of the best aspects of pre-*Beyond the Fringe* stage revue. I've said before that I felt revue never really adapted to environments other than the stage, and these series did little to change my mind, though it was good to have a new television audience for 'Siren Song', and I loved joining my old friend Dilys Laye in a performance of a song that had featured in a revue called *Ten Years Hard* about how Islington had become gentrified.

I landed a rare serious role in the television play *That Old Black Magic*, broadcast in February 1967 and based on a similar idea to that behind the film *Guess Who's Coming to Dinner* – middle-class white girl falls for black man and has to overcome the resistance of her family. I was the mother and George Cole was the father, with Julia Foster as our daughter and Johnny Sekka as the black lodger, and the play made its point very strongly, showing up the innate prejudice of the white parents in a way that nowadays might be considered deeply politically incorrect – as, for example, in my asking the young black man in a very pointed manner: 'What sort of things do you eat?'

*Carry On Doctor*, the second of the series to be set in a hospital, was released in 1967. I played Chloe Gibson, dowdy assistant of the bogus faith healer Mr Bigger, played by yet another actor I'd worked with years ago, Frankie Howerd. Chloe is extremely hard of hearing, and towards the end of the film she is married to Mr Bigger by the chaplain (Peter Jones), who similarly suffers from deafness. For some reason – probably the simple one that it was an extremely funny scene – every time Frankie and I acted the marriage ceremony we would disintegrate into fits of giggles, and our laughter was so infectious that it instantly spread to the crew, which caused such a racket that before we knew it the set was being invaded by actors and technicians shooting other films at Pinewood who wanted to know what was causing all this mirth. Frankie jokingly put all the blame on me: after the fifth take in a row had been ruined by our descending into hysterics, he pleaded to Gerry Thomas: 'I need a couple of Valium before I come on the set with this woman!'

*Doctor* was the first of Frankie's two *Carry On*s. Although he didn't go down well with everyone on the team – Kenneth Williams was very snide in his diaries, describing him as 'undoubtedly a very boring man' – I was a terrific admirer. I found him a wonderful actor to work with and equally wonderful company off the set.

One year we did a television show together, and before the recording I calmed my nerves by putting away a large plate of my favourite delicacy at the time: egg and chips. After the show Frankie suggested we have dinner, but I declined on account of the egg and chips. I really wasn't hungry, I said, but I'd go with him for a quick drink. We went to the Belvedere, a lovely restaurant in Holland Park, where the delicious cooking smells and the effect of a couple of vodka and tonics renewed my appetite, and I suggested that I might just manage a little something after all. I ended up consuming a full three-course dinner, and when Frankie saw the bill he commented drily: 'If this is what you cost me when you're not hungry, Joan, I'd hate to take you out when you've got an appetite.'

The more I got to work with Frankie the more closely I came to know him – but that was still not very closely at all. There was a part of him that was impenetrable, locked away in the furthest recesses of his personality. To the outside world he was a wonderfully funny man, but I could never get much sense of what was going on inside. And, as was often the case with solo comics when they join an existing company of actors, Frankie was not really a team player. All those years ago he'd been upstaging me in our *High Spirits* turn in the Royal Variety Show, and a similar slipping of discipline when working with other actors – not thinking of the other person's timing, getting in the way of their delivery – was occasionally evident when he acted in *Carry On* films.

But one look from that sad, sad face and I could forgive Frankie anything.

After *Doctor* came what remains to many connoisseurs of the series, and to most of the actors and production staff, the best of all the *Carry On* films: *Carry On Up the Khyber*.

Jim Dale was not available, so the handsome male lead role was taken by Roy Castle, in his one and only *Carry On* appearance: he was a delight to work with, and I only wish I had got to act with him more. Most of the other regulars were in the film – Sid was my husband Sir Sidney Ruff-Diamond, Kenny Williams was Randi Lal, the Khazi of Kalabar, Charlie Hawtrey was Private

James Widdle, Bernard Bresslaw was Bungdit Din – and with a brilliant script by Tolly Rothwell, everything just fell into place. (An added bonus was that *Chitty Chitty Bang Bang* was being filmed at Pinewood at the same time as we were making *Khyber*, and it was a terrific thrill to meet one of the great international stars, Dick Van Dyke.)

The Khyber Pass sequences were shot on location in Snowdonia, a place which, while undeniably spectacular, did nothing for me at all. I've always suffered from a fear of heights, and being perched on the side of a mountain was not exactly my idea of fun. We were billeted in a very fine hotel, but the trip up the mountain every morning in a little jeep scared the life out of me, and I arrived on the set a gibbering wreck: I had to position my chair facing the mountainside as I couldn't bear to look down!

One of my big moments in *Khyber* had me lying on a divan, wearing a dress that the Khazi has just given me. The Khazi, who has left the room, returns:

*Lady Ruff-Diamond:* I thought you'd forgotten all about me.
*Khazi:* Impossible, my dear madam.
*Lady R-D:* You haven't mentioned the dress.
*Khazi:* Sari.
*Lady R-D:* There's no need to apologise. There's a nice little fringe . . .
*Khazi:* No no no, the garment is called a sari.

186

*Lady R-D:* Oh yes, of course, silly me – the sari with the fringe on top!

While Kenny and I were shooting this scene, he suddenly broke wind in the most appallingly noisy and smelly manner. Kenny was noted for his bouts of flatulence – he suffered constantly from problems in his digestive system – but even by his standards this was a real corker. The crew collapsed on the floor in giggles, and Gerry Thomas called for a hasty cut as I remonstrated with my co-actor.

'Kenneth – how can we play this scene when you keep farting?'

As usual he had a quick response.

'Well – Rudolph Valentino used to fart!'

'Yes,' butted in Gerry, quick as flash, 'but they were silent films.'

The most enduring scene of *Up the Khyber* – indeed, probably the most famous scene in any *Carry On* film – was the dinner party in which the British rulers in India show themselves the very model of Stiff Upper Lip-ness by continuing with their dinner while their compound is under siege from native marauders. Shells explode all around them, the orchestra is wiped out, the ceiling falls in – but still the Brits carry on eating in a dignified and proper manner.

The idea of the scene was very funny, but its execution was far from simple, and it took three days to shoot – an amazingly long time for any *Carry On* episode. First the whole scene was filmed as a master shot, and then Gerry Thomas would concentrate on close-ups. On the second day, with the master shot safely in the can, we made our way back on to the set, picking our way through the chaos of food, mud and rubble (Fuller's Earth playing the part of debris). During one of my own close-ups, chunks of the dining-room ceiling landed in my hair, and my ad-libbed reaction – 'Oh dear, I seem to have got a little plastered!' – was kept in the film.

Appreciation of *Carry On Up the Khyber* was not confined to devoted fans of the series. When in September 1999 the British Film Institute polled its members about their one hundred favourite feature films of the century, *Khyber* proudly found its way on to the roll of honour – in ninety-ninth place, one ahead of *The Killing Fields*.

It was back to hospital for *Carry On Again, Doctor*, in which I played the wealthy Mrs Ellen Moore – a rather humdrum name in a film where Jim Dale was Dr James Nookey, Sid James was Gladstone Screwer, Charlie Hawtrey was Dr Ernest Stoppidge and Kenneth Williams played the surgeon Dr Carver.

Shooting of *Carry On Camping* began in October 1968, a time of year far from ideal for a film which involved so many outdoor scenes played in shorts and camping wear. We found our-selves speaking most of our lines through chattering teeth, but needs must, and it turned out to be one of the most enjoyable of the series to make. After a barrage of complaints from the actors that we had nowhere to warm up between takes than the few canvas chairs set outside in about six inches of mud, we were eventually supplied with a caravan, into which we all piled in an effort to get warm. Outside, meanwhile, the Pinewood mud, which served as the campsite, was being sprayed green to give the impression of lush grassland, and the leaves which had fallen off the trees were being doggedly stuck back to make the landscape look like summer. At one point there was even a flurry of snow, which threatened to interrupt filming, but cameraman Ernest Steward kept rolling: 'We'll pretend it's blossom.'

Most of all I remember the cold – the bitter, all-embracing cold. To look as if we were enjoying a camping holiday in the summer – that was *real* acting.

*Carry On Up the Jungle*, next in the series, brought me more hilarity with Frankie Howerd. He was Professor Inigo Tinkle and I was Lady Evelyn Bagley:

*Tinkle:* Did you see the giraffes just now?
*Bagley:* Yes I did. Quaint things. I wonder why it is they have such long necks.
*Tinkle:* That's quite simple. It's because their heads are so far away from their bodies.

I found it impossible to get out my line without cracking up, and after a few takes this was beginning to stretch Gerry Thomas's patience. Next time I tried everything I could think of to control myself

189

– gloomy thoughts, pushing my fingernails into my palms – and eventually we got the exchange right, but it was a close thing, and very symptomatic of working with Frankie. That hang-dog expression of his just had me in stitches.

A very different problem for me in *Up the Jungle* was my nude scene. One day Lady Bagley takes a shower at the makeshift encampment deep in the jungle – which generates no end of interest from Professor Tinkle and the other men on the expedition. The script stipulated a nude shot of me in the shower, leered over by Claude Chumley (Kenny Connor) from his vantage point up a tree and, for good measure, a gorilla who has climbed into the tree alongside Chumley to get a better view. Try as I might, I couldn't bring myself to do that nude shot. As usual I was feeling overweight and it just didn't feel right. I suggested to Gerry Thomas that I wear a body stocking, but he insisted – rightly – that everyone would realise it was a body stocking, and the joke would be lost.

It was usually the case that any nude – or near-nude – scene would have people crowding on to the gantry for a good look, and that happened now; but even after Gerry had cleared the set I just couldn't bring myself to do it. He was very understanding, and in the end a thinner and younger version of Lady Bagley was substituted for that shot. I shouldn't think the red-blooded young men in cinemas around the world complained.

*Up the Jungle* was released in 1970, and later the same year along came *Carry On Loving*, which was never one of my favourites – perhaps because I had to play a character named Esme Crowfoot. The plot revolved around the Wedded Bliss dating agency run by Sid and Hattie; Kenneth Williams played Percival Snooper, a marriage guidance counsellor himself in need of professional marriage guidance. Little did I suspect when making comic business with Kenny about the pitfalls of wedlock that before long he would be proposing marriage to me . . .

Kenny and I would often spend time together nattering off the set at Pinewood, and after a while had become fairly close. But I was still taken aback by the turn that one of our conversations took. He had come to my dressing room between takes, and we were putting the world to rights when he started coming to the point.

'So how's your private life?'

This was a time well beyond Tony Baird and John Walters, so I was telling the truth when I replied: 'Not much happening – probably about the same as yours.'

'Don't talk to me about that. My career's all right, but I've made a bloody mess of my private life. But you – you're constantly sitting there waiting for this prince on a white charger to gallop up and whisk you away. It's not going to happen.'

'No,' I replied, 'but one can remain optimistic.'

I could tell that he was getting at something, and suddenly he came out with it.

'You and I – we'd make the most wonderful

couple. We'd give fabulous parties – we'd be the talk of the town.'

There was a short silence as this started to sink in, and then he continued: 'Let's get married.'

I was reeling from this suggestion when he made an even more preposterous one: 'I'd give you a child if you wanted one.' And then the small print: 'I'd want to carry on leading my own life, though: we couldn't sleep together after that.'

I realised that this was not being said in a light-hearted way, and started to feel very embarrassed by the confrontation. Fond as I was of Kenny, the very notion of living with him was outrageous: I'd have been worn out by lunchtime on the first day!

But he was waiting for a reaction.

'Well, what do you think?'

I was dumbfounded, and scarcely knew what to say. I had no desire to hurt his feelings, but the idea of marrying him was bizarre. Kenny, of course, was widely known to be gay, and while I had no problem with that – I'd long been aware that many of my closest male friends were gay, and took pride in describing myself as a Queens' Pudding – as far as the idea of being married to him was concerned . . . Please, God, no!

So there I was thinking: how am I going to get out of this?

I could see that he was quite serious, and to cover my confusion blurted out: 'Thanks, Kenny darling, but what's in it for me?'

At this the old Kenneth Williams suddenly snapped back into place. 'Oh, nothing but sand!'

No, I don't know what he meant either, but the tension was broken: we both burst out laughing, and the subject was never broached again.

Kenny was certainly the most complex character – and at the same time the most talented, most imaginative, most intellectual actor – with whom I worked regularly. He was not difficult to get on with when performing a show or filming a scene, but he could be maddening off the set, and the trouble was that it was impossible to predict his mood.

During the filming of *Carry On – Don't Lose Your Head*, Norah Holland's husband 'Dutch' came down to visit the set with his mother, who was a great fan of Kenny's and was particularly keen to meet him. So I went into Kenny's dressing room to tell him they were coming, only to be sent away with a flea in my ear: 'No, no, I don't want to meet them,' he announced imperiously.

'You're an evil little bastard!' I scolded him, but by then he was set in his mood and was determined not to change his mind.

For the next three days he refused to speak to me, sinking into that childish grump which was all too often his characteristic demeanour. That was one of Kenny's most exasperating features: once he had worked himself into a difficult mood, he thought it a sign of weakness to mellow, so just got more and more entrenched, and as often as not you simply didn't know what had upset his applecart.

The next day we had to share a car to be driven

to Waddesdon Manor in Buckinghamshire for a location shoot, and Kenny made sure that he sat in the front and I in the back. For the entire hour of the journey he spoke not a single word to me. When we arrived on the set Gerry Thomas and Peter Rogers were waiting for us.

'And how's my darling girl this morning?' asked Gerry.

'Fine – but I'd be even better if my co-star here would deign to talk to me' – and I explained the business about Norah's mother-in-law and how Kenny had taken umbrage at being told off. Gerry and Peter were never ones to let problems between their actors fester – there simply wasn't time for such distractions – and they took Kenny off into a corner for a quiet word. Exactly what that word was I never asked, but it did the trick: when we started shooting the scene, which involved our getting out of the carriage on arrival at Sir Rodney Ffing's ball (yes, the very one where dear Elspeth March tells Sid James, 'You've always had magnificent balls'), Kenny made a point of throwing his cloak around me, oozing, 'Come on, I can't have my darling one getting cold.'

There was no sarcasm in this. The whole problem was over, and after that he was always absolutely charming to Dutch, but a little while later I was telling Peter Butterworth about this episode, and he made an astute observation: 'The trouble with Kenny is that he's just like a little schoolboy. He does something and he knows he's gone too far, but he just doesn't know how to say sorry.'

There was another spat during the filming of *Carry On Camping*. A lovely young actress named Elizabeth Knight was taking her first *Carry On* role as one of Barbara Windsor's schoolmates, and understandably she felt nervous about joining an established team of well-known actors. Most of us were very welcoming to newcomers, and on her first day on the set I invited her to come to the restaurant with me at lunchtime: if the rest of the gang met her at lunch, it would be much easier for her to work with them in the afternoon.

As we entered the restaurant I spied Kenny sitting at our usual table all on his own, delicately dissecting his trout (as was his habit). We went over to sit down with him, and as we reached the table he puffed himself up, glared at Liz and announced: 'You can't sit down here. This is reserved for the *Carry On* team.'

I explained as patiently as I could that Liz *was* part of the *Carry On* team for that film, but this didn't wash: 'No no!' he ranted. 'This table is for the *regular* team.'

Pausing only to tell him, 'You are a demonic little sod!' I led Liz away and we went and sat elsewhere. Kenny refused to speak to me for the rest of the day, but the following morning acted as if nothing had happened.

Just occasionally I'd try to get my own back on Kenny for his petulant behaviour. I'd heard that early in his career he'd appeared in the film of *The Beggar's Opera*, starring Laurence Olivier, and his voice had been dubbed by another actor. Kenny was still very sensitive about what he considered a slight on his talents, and I decided to play a little trick on him.

Once he had filmed his scenes, Kenny showed little interest in the result, and rarely watched the rushes. I thought I'd take advantage of this, and one day on the set took him on one side.

'Sid has told me what's happened, and I just want to say that I think it's disgusting.'

He looked at me as if I were mad. 'What's disgusting?'

'You mean you haven't been round to the dubbing suite?'

'The dubbing suite? Why should I want to go round to the dubbing suite?'

'Oh, Kenny, I'm so sorry. I thought you knew. Anyway, I just want you to know that Sid and I both think it's so unfair.'

Suddenly he latched on, and those great nostrils started flaring as only Kenny's could.

'Joan – you've been a good friend to me, and if there's something I should know, then you must tell me.'

'Well . . . Gerald has been watching the last few days' worth of rushes and apparently he isn't happy with your performance. He thinks you've been camping it up far too much. But it's too late to reshoot, so this morning he's brought in another actor to dub over all your scenes.'

Poor Kenny. It was the first time I'd ever seen him speechless – but not for long. He went storming over to Gerald and started yelling at him: 'How dare you? How dare you desecrate my art? When you dub over my voice you destroy the finest part of my work . . .'

Gerald let him rage away for another half a minute, then gently put his hand on Kenny's shoulder and turned him round to face where Sid and I were watching this display – creased up laughing. Kenny knew he'd been had.

Away from the set, Kenny could put aside all the camping around and become a very different character. He had not enjoyed a particularly good education but had a true passion for learning and an astonishing brain, and it was mesmerising to sit and listen to him expound on all sorts of subjects: art, literature, philosophy, politics – you name it, Kenny could lecture on it. Most of this talk went way over my head, but it was fascinating to witness him in full flood.

Also fascinating, on a rather different level, were his twin obsessions with privacy and hygiene. He hated people visiting him at his flat, and if someone did manage to find their way over the drawbridge, he invariably refused to let them anywhere near his loo. I managed the first, but I never did achieve the second.

One day Kenny, Hattie and I shared a car back from Pinewood. When we arrived outside his flat near Great Portland Street he was all ready to scuttle in and regain his priceless privacy, but Hattie and I had other thoughts.

'Right, Kenny – we're coming in for a cup of tea.'

'Ooh, no – you can't do that. I never let anybody in there.'

Hattie was very firm: 'We're coming in, Kenneth. No arguments.'

Unsurprisingly, the combined weight of Hattie and myself prevailed, and Kenny reluctantly led the way up to his little flat. It was furnished in an extraordinary way. The sitting room was almost totally bare: there was no television (if he wanted to watch a programme he'd go next door to his mother's flat), and just about the only item of furniture was a lectern in the middle of the room. The walls were lined with hundreds of books but there were no other personal items of any sort: no pictures, no ornaments. It was almost like a hospital ward, so clinical was its mood, but to Kenny it was a haven, and while I hardly ever saw him quiet in public, I could imagine that this was where he found his peace.

One area of his flat, as I say, remained resolutely out of bounds.

'You can't use my lavatory!' he insisted, and we could only reply with: 'We don't want to use your bloody lavatory!' I suppose one of us could have distracted him while the other sneaked in there for a peep, but that would have been grossly unfair to him. We'd got behind the outer barrier, and that was enough.

Away from the *Carry On* films, Kenny and I were involved in several projects together. There was no better example of the way we seemed to respond instinctively to each other than *A Tribute to Greatness*, three radio programmes scripted by Myles Rudge and broadcast in 1967 on what was then the Third Programme (now Radio Three), a very highbrow home for comedy. (Myles told me that they were the first original comedy programmes ever broadcast on that network.) Each programme was a hilarious spoof documentary on a different towering cultural icon. 'A Bannister Called Freda' concerned the search for the singer Freda Bannister, 'A Strolling Player Looks Back' was about the great thespian Plantagenet Runciman, and 'Twilight at the Athelstan' was an elegiac portrait of the faded glory of the Athelstan Hotel. Kenny deployed the full and extraordinary range of his voices in the male roles, while I had all the female parts and John Moffatt was the indefatigable and long-suffering reporter. I got to sing some wonderful cod-Victorian songs (written by Ted Dicks) with titles like 'I Search for Blossoms in Life's Garden' and 'Blow Out the Light, Beloved', which had Kenny in stitches – and one newspaper commenting that I should be enlisted to sing 'Rule Britannia' at the Last Night of the Proms in the Royal Albert Hall. That would have been quite a sight!

But my big chance to work even more often with Kenny was tragically thwarted.

Towards the end of 1968 I was asked if I'd be interested in joining the team on that wonderful radio series *Round the Horne*. It had been running for years and had a huge following, with the team of Kenneth Horne, Kenneth Williams, Hugh

Paddick, Bill Pertwee and Betty Marsden, and writers Barry Took and Marty Feldman, providing one of the most popular – and funniest – radio shows ever broadcast. Betty, with whom I had worked in revue years earlier and who had been in two *Carry On* films (*Regardless* and *Camping*), had decided to leave the show, and I was considered the ideal replacement. What an opportunity!

I was all ready to start work on recording the new series, and had even been photographed with Kenneth Horne, Hugh Paddick, Bill Pertwee and Kenny for the front cover of *Radio Times*. Then, in February 1969, came the devastating news: Kenneth Horne had died suddenly, and obviously the new series was abandoned. That photo-shoot with Kenneth Horne was, sadly, the only time I ever met him.

(This was not the first time that plans for me to join forces with a famous comedy team had been so sadly thwarted. In 1965 I had acted with Arthur Haynes in *Doctor in Clover*, and afterwards heard from Peter Eade that Arthur wanted me to join his highly successful television show. This was wonderful news – but before we could start work Arthur, a lovely man, very different off-screen from his curmudgeonly on-screen persona, had died suddenly at the absurdly early age of fifty-two.)

Within a very short time after Kenneth Horne's death a plan had been hatched for a new programme along similar lines, to be fronted by Kenny. This was originally to be called *It's Bold* (echoing a constant refrain from the Julian and

Sandy episodes in *Round the Horne*), but ended up taking its name from another of Kenny's ringing catchphrases and became *Stop Messing About*, with a first series running from March until June 1969. The show was co-written by my old mate Myles Rudge, and Hugh Paddick and I were supporting Kenny. I had some great characters to play, such as Maud Neversole: 'Doesn't the fishmonger have cold hands? It's because he's been handling fish all day.'

The trouble with *Stop Messing About* was that it was not – and could never be – *Round the Horne*, and without Kenneth Horne as a figure of authority around which the comedy could flow there would never be the same rock-solid core to the show. Kenny certainly felt this, and was constantly in a state of panic about whether his own personality could sustain the show, and whether his outrageous characters and constant innuendo were as effective without Kenneth Horne to bounce them off. I never felt that Kenny's heart was completely in *Stop Messing About*, and was not too surprised that the show ran for only two series.

But Kenny and I had got on so well on the radio series that I was delighted to be asked to join him in *The Kenneth Williams Show* on BBC television. This was a wonderful series to be part of: I was a real co-star, the scripts – written mostly by Kenneth himself and John Law – were first-rate, and I loved the routine of meeting up with Kenny and with the producer Roger Ordish half an hour before we were due to start rehearsing so that Kenny could regale us with his views on everything under the sun. We'd hang on his every word: though self-taught, he had an amazing range of knowledge, and would have made a superb teacher. (Sadly, John Law died during the recording of the second series.)

On *The Kenneth Williams Show* Kenny would introduce me with the words, 'With a great deal of respect and not a little warmth', and one of my most cherished possessions is a large plate which he presented to me at the end of the series in February 1970, inscribed: 'With a great deal of respect & not a little warmth to a very nice person'.

That plate is a charming souvenir of one of my greatest friends, but another precious possession is perhaps a more characteristic reminder of this extraordinary man.

Kenny was in great demand to make personal appearances and, being assiduous about responding to such requests, he had had printed a card that read:

Mr Kenneth Williams thanks you for your letter, but regrets that because of other engagements he is unable to accept your invitation.

I have one of these cards, in an envelope which he addressed to 'Miss Joan Sims (née Bagwash)'. Sent to me in April 1970, it has been amended in Kenny's handwriting to read:

Mr Kenneth Williams thanks you for your suggestion, but regrets that because of other engagements he is unable to accept your invitation to a cheap lunch next Wednesday & says you can stick it up your arse.
love
K.

# 7

# . . . And Carrying On Carrying On

Twenty *Carry On* films down, and who knew how many to go?

By now the routine was pretty well established. I'd hear from Peter Eade that another film was being scheduled, and about a month before shooting began the script would arrive. This would usually be the cue for me to ring Hattie.

'Are we really going to do this again?'

'Of course we are, darling.'

'Same old jokes.'

'I know, darling, but won't it be fun?'

And, of course, it was.

First thing to do was read the script and learn the part. I still underlined all my own lines in red ink, then spoke them very slowly on to a tape so that I could play them back to myself as I pottered around the house. Putting in the inflexion and expression could come later: the first priority was the words themselves.

The next big moment would be the costume

fitting – which for a long time meant being bunged into a taxi and driven round to Bermans, the theatrical outfitters. Being fitted for a costume had long been a major hang-up for me, a part of making a film that would always get me fretting. I was not, by this time, a lady of what you might call regular proportions, and as I've mentioned before many of the costumes I ended up with would have been used in some previous production and adapted for my own dimensions by the insertion of a panel of material into the back. So having a costume made specifically for me – as happened more and more as my career advanced – was a special joy. All the costume designers' skills were brought to the fore, and those skills are rarely considered by film-goers. It's quite miraculous what a top costume designer like Sonia Kerr – who worked on the Dick Emery shows – can do with a couple of bits of braid: Sonia used to design my dresses so that they had a little line of fabric on either side of the centre front, which made me look half the size on camera. There are other tricks of the trade – stand-out pockets, for example, make you look slimmer – and I was in need of them all. Once it was a case of having a costume designed for me, rather than my being packed off to Bermans for a bit up the back, I became far less conscious of my weight.

After the costume fitting it was off to try on a few wigs, and I was all set.

There was no such thing as a read-through, and the actors were expected to be DLP (dead letter perfect) by the time we assembled at Pinewood at crack of dawn for the first day of shooting. Get hair pinned up and go along to be made up; have hair done; then slip into costume and be on the set by eight-thirty. General hellos, and we were ready for work.

We'd run through the scene a couple of times and then repair to our dressing rooms while the stage was lit, with stand-ins taking up the actors' positions so that all the technical creases could be ironed out before we came back for the shoot.

The *Carry On* films were blessed with an ultra-professional crew, which was essential given the extreme constraints of time – each one was filmed in six weeks, and not a minute more – and the crew soon became good friends of the actors. Lighting cameraman Alan Hume, for example, worked on half of my twenty-four *Carry On* films and was an essential part of the series' success. All the ladies loved him: he took great pains to show us in the very best possible way. Alan was also one of the world's great gigglers, and since for a *Carry On* film the crew was the audience, it was reassuring to hear him chortling away. In terms of making the film, of course, it was less useful, and he used to stuff a gigantic handkerchief into his mouth to stifle his laughs while the cameras were rolling.

Laughter on the set was an occupational hazard of making the *Carry On*s, but sometimes it went too far. There was a carpenter known as Whiplash who used to watch the filming perched on a gantry, and he showed his appreciation with a wheezy sort of laugh which made him sound like a constipated hyena. One day this noise just got too much for Gerry Thomas, who had to ask him – ever so politely – to leave the set while the scene was being shot.

Gerry himself was a marvel. Despite the unrelenting pressure of time under which he worked, I never once saw him lose his temper or even raise his voice, and it was he who set the mood that pervaded every *Carry On* set: very relaxed, but very disciplined. We all thought the world of him, not least because he was a complete pro and he wanted us to behave with equal professionalism. He had made his way up the directing ranks from working in the cutting room through a spell as an editor, and had a real knack of knowing exactly what each shot should look like by the time he arrived on the set. No messing about – we got straight on with it. Very few scenes needed more than two takes, and very little was left on the cutting-room floor. When you consider that Gerry directed every frame of every one of the thirty *Carry On* films, it's no exaggeration to say that he was more important to the series than any other single individual.

Rushes of the previous day's filming were shown at lunchtime, when I and a few of the other actors would cut short our meal to go to the rushes theatre and see how the scene had come out. For me this was essentially an educational experience: I would mentally be giving myself notes about how the scene had played, how I might do something better or otherwise differently, and generally finding out what I could about my own acting technique. (Quite early in my film career I noticed that I had a bad habit when talking with another actor of looking from one eye to the other, which was distracting. So I trained myself always to look at the eye nearer the camera.)

In the rushes theatre I always had one ear cocked towards what Gerry was saying to the other members of the crew as he watched: that way I could learn how others were reacting to a particular performance.

Watching with Gerry could also mean making the occasional plea to be shown in a better light than might have been the case. When I saw the rushes of the scene in *Khyber* where Roy Castle, Charlie Hawtrey and I dress up as belly dancers, I was horrified at my appearance: fat tummy, nasty thick waist – my worst fears about my appearance were confirmed, especially when I came up against the gorgeous figure of Angela Douglas. I took Gerry on one side and explained that I thought I looked hideous. 'Don't worry, darling, I'll see what I can do' – and he must have done something very clever, as in the final version of the scene I don't look nearly as bad as I'd thought. It just goes to show what a top-class film editor can do.

At the end of the six weeks we'd disperse – to other films, or television, or the stage – until the next time. We never all sat down to watch the finished product together, and to this day I have never seen a *Carry On* film in the cinema – indeed, there are some *Carry On* films which I wasn't in

My agent Peter Eade with three of his protégés – Kenneth Williams, yours truly and Ronnie Barker – and his faithful assistant, Laurena Dewar.

*Carry On Cowboy* – 'So you're Belle...' 'Yeah. My intimate friends call me Ding Dong.' With Sid James and Percy Herbert.

Aquarius/Canal + Image UK Ltd

*Carry On Doctor* – Frankie Howerd in need of another Valium.

© Carlton International

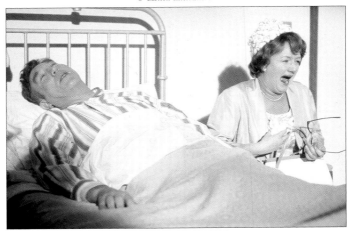

*Carry On Up the Khyber* – 'Oh dear, I seem to have got a little plastered!' With Roy Castle.

© Carlton International

*Carry On Again, Doctor* – getting down to business with Charlie Hawtrey.

© Carlton International

*Carry On Camping* – another shocking scene with Hattie.
Photo BFI Stills, Posters and Designs © Carlton International

*Carry On Henry* – Kenny overcome by the garlic.

*Four of my favourite
television comedies:*

LEFT: With Victoria
Wood and Celia Imrie
in *The Victoria Wood
Show*.
BBC Picture Archives

BELOW: With Dennis
Waterman in *On the Up*.
BBC Picture Archives

OPPOSITE TOP: With
Richard Pearson and
George Cole in
*My Good Friend*.
© Anglia Television Ltd

OPPOSITE BOTTOM: With
Frank Middlemass,
Judi Dench and
Geoffrey Palmer in
*As Time Goes By*.
BBC Picture Archives

OVERLEAF: 'Sad we have to get old, isn't it?' – as Betsy Prig in *Martin Chuzzlewit*. BBC Picture Archives

which I've never seen at all. There was never a glamorous West End première at which we could all turn up dripping with jewels, with our devoted fans held back behind the crush barriers, but never mind: it was the box office that mattered, not giving the actors their moment of glory and glamour.

The backroom people on the *Carry On*s were wonderful. Our make-up team was usually Geoff Rodway and his wife Nora, and I can vividly remember them larking around with Bernard Bresslaw during the making of *Carry On Cowboy*. Bernie was playing a Red Indian named Little Heap, and applying all the body make-up to his giant figure was quite a task – so Nora commandeered a step ladder and made Bernie stand stock still while she climbed up to get access to his more remote bits!

I had – and still have – a very special friendship with my stand-in Norah Holland. Norah first worked with me early in the *Carry On* series (neither she nor I chooses to remember exactly how early) and she soon became a regular member of the team. She was, in the nicest sense, one of the lads, and enthusiastically joined in the poker school which Sid James, Charlie Hawtrey and Bernard Bresslaw set up between takes. 'Got the necessary?' Sid would always ask Norah as soon as she arrived, and invariably she had: out came her little table and chair and her pack of cards, the hands were dealt and away they went. They played only for sixpences and shillings, but it was an excellent way of filling in the spare time that filming inevitably involves, and although I was not a great card player myself, I joined in whenever I could.

It wasn't only as organiser of the poker school that Norah was indispensable. She used to keep Peter Rogers supplied with jelly babies, and whenever we fancied bacon and mushroom sandwiches during an early call she'd take our orders and be off to the canteen to collect them. Crammed with bacon and dripping in butter, this delicacy, the speciality of the Pinewood canteen, became the staple diet of most of the *Carry On* team, and if the craving for bacon and mushroom sandwiches coincided with when she should have been standing in for me the sandwiches would take priority, and I'd have to go and be my own stand-in.

The rapture with which I'd tuck myself away to consume my bacon and mushroom sandwiches became something of a standing joke on the *Carry On* set. One morning I went back with my haul to my little hideaway in a darkened area away from the main stage. I sat down and unwrapped my first sandwich, and was halfway through it when suddenly I was bathed in light: all the arc lamps on the set had been trained on that table, and as my expression switched from the rapture of scoffing that sandwich to bewilderment at what was going on, the stills photographer appeared and started clicking away. I'd been set up!

Norah had first made a name for herself in the film business as a stunt driver – she drove for Julie

Christie in *The Fast Lady* – and her extensive experience included doubling for Shelley Winters in *Lolita*. Her husband Les – 'Dutch' – was an airline pilot, and her availability to come and be my stand-in always depended on whether she was about to jet off with him to some exotic place. It struck me as deeply ironic that my stand-in would drive to Pinewood in her husband's Daimler Sovereign, wear a mink coat and get to go on all those fancy cruises, while the star had to make do with a Triumph Herald and some manky old fur fabric.

Had appearing in *Carry On* films been a more lucrative business, maybe I'd have been going on those cruises with her, but pay was a constant bugbear for all the actors. At the peak of the series the leading men were earning £5,000 per film, but the leading ladies – Barbara, Hattie and myself – were getting exactly half that: the princely sum of £2,500, the very same that I'd earned for *Carry On Nurse* back in 1959, and for *Teacher* the same year. For each of the great ones like *Cleo* and *Khyber* I earned £2,500. And when I made *Carry On Emmanuelle* in 1978, my last Carry On film nearly two decades after my first, I earned . . . well, go on, guess.

The concept of inflation simply didn't register as far as our paymasters were concerned, and the fact that most of the technicians were earning more than we were did not make us any less restive. Moaning to Peter Rogers never got us anywhere. The *Carry On*s were produced to a very tight budget, he'd say, and there was no more money in the kitty. Nor do any of the main actors who are still alive today – sadly, all too few – benefit to the tune of a single penny from the constant re-runs of *Carry On* films on television in Britain and around the world, nor any of the endless compilations that have been spun out of the series. Peter Rogers's quip that 'I'll do anything for my actors except pay them' wears a bit thin when you see *Carry On* film after *Carry On* film in the daily television listings and you know you're not getting any benefit; and his avowal that 'I only pay my actors what I think they are worth' just rubs salt into the wound.

Early in 2000 Peter wrote in the *Mail on Sunday*:

We had modest budgets and I made a film for the money some people would spend on a set for one scene.

I decided that to keep down budget levels it would be an idea if the artists formed a kind of repertory – which they were anyway – and took percentages of the films' profits. But their agents said No.

If they had taken percentages the artists would have been very wealthy today and would still be getting cheques through the post. The only two who admitted their refusal was a mistake were Kenneth Williams, who thought they ought to have accepted, and Barbara Windsor, who is always moaning that every time the films appear on television she does not get anything out of them.

He's certainly right that they were made to tight budgets: *Carry On Sergeant* reputedly cost about £70,000 to make – absolute peanuts, even by the standard of those days – and the most expensive, *Carry On Henry*, a mere £250,000. All made a profit except *Carry On Columbus*.

But I never heard any of the actors talk of that proposed profit-sharing venture, and my agent Peter Eade would certainly have told me had any such proposition been made to him with regard to me. If it was, I knew nothing of it, and nor did his assistant Laurena Dewar.

But I don't want to be bracketed with Babs Windsor as a moaner, and in any case, I wasn't exactly staring poverty in the face during the hey-day of the *Carry On* series. After all, I had been doing well enough to buy my parents a house not far from Laindon in Southchurch. My mother continued to live there after my father's death, and I saw as much of her as I could.

Although the big bust-up between myself and my mother had long been laid to rest, there was still an undercurrent of dissatisfaction in her attitude towards me, and sometimes I felt that in her eyes I could never do anything exactly right.

If I was having a drink or two she'd pointedly say, 'Well, at least I know when *I*'ve had enough . . .' If I was going out for the evening and asked her how I looked, it would always be: 'You look lovely, but . . .' and she'd find some little fault with what I was wearing.

Nor was she entirely satisfied with how my

213

career was going. She was delighted by my success, but she constantly wanted me to be doing something a little more upmarket. 'Do you have to be doing those *Carry On*s?' she'd say. 'Couldn't you get into something better?' She was certainly proud of me, but had rather a funny way of showing it.

After my father's death I tried to take my mother on holiday as often as I could, and one year she and her friend Mrs Collins – whose husband owned the ironmonger's shop at Laindon – joined myself, Myles Rudge and Peter Eade's assistant Laurena for a skiing holiday in Switzerland. None of us had ever skied before, and I did not take to it at all, but my great memory of that holiday is of Mrs Collins giving her verdict on the food: at every meal she'd announce, in a tone of dire warning, 'It's reheated meat, Gladys! It's reheated meat!'

Team spirit among the *Carry On* gang was fabled, but naturally I became closer to some of the actors than others.

Hattie Jacques was like a combination of sister and mother to me. I'd often spend Christmas at her home, and they were the best Christmases I've ever known. Nothing was ever too much trouble for her, and she soon became – and was to remain – one of my closest friends and one of the great props of my life.

Of the men, only Kenny Williams ever went so far as to propose to me, but I did have a very soft spot for them all, and in particular for dear old

214

Charles Hawtrey. Charlie was an intensely proud man, who had been making films since before I was born. He'd acted with the likes of Will Hay, but he clearly revelled in the atmosphere at Pinewood, and any film without Charlie in it wasn't quite the same. I can still see him getting stuck into the poker school, with his funny little habit of standing his cigarette on end on the table as he played his hand. He was a wicked corpser, too, and in my scene with him in the arbour in *Don't Lose Your Head* took great delight in looking mischievously at me as I delivered the line, 'My brother – the Count – wishes to meet him,' with the result that I could scarcely stop myself cracking up while still in shot.

Notoriously eccentric, his air of pervasive sadness was not helped by his fondness for the occasional Wincarnis – a handy euphemism for alcohol coined by my old friend the singer David Kernan after the tonic wine – and this eventually made it impossible for him to go on working in the *Carry On* films. We kept in close touch, though, after he had retired to live on the coast in Sussex, and his convoluted telephone calls became a regular feature of Sunday afternoons. The phone would ring, I'd pick it up, and there would be that unforgettable voice:

'Aaah . . . Hello, darling . . . Aaah . . .'

'What are you up to, Charles?'

'Aah . . . Darling girl . . . Aaah . . . Mmm . . .'

He'd go on in this vein for about half an hour, and then his conversation (if you can call it that) would peter out altogether and he'd hang up – probably to go and get himself a refill.

If Kenneth Williams's flat was remarkable for its sparseness, Charlie's was quite the opposite. It was chaos, with pieces of furniture stacked halfway up each wall. Charlie's greatest love was his cat, and every day at Pinewood he'd nip off to the canteen to scrounge food for it.

Special Constable Gorse, inseparable from his budgie Bobby in *Constable*; Dan Dann the Lavatory Man in *Screaming!*; the Duc de Pommfrit in *Don't Lose Your Head*; Mr Barron, enduring a sympathetic pregnancy in *Doctor*; Private James Widdle in *Up the Khyber*: poor Charlie was a very lonely and very mixed-up little man, but the *Carry On* films would not have been the same without him.

My own favourite among Charlie's *Carry On* roles was Sir Roger de Lodgerley in *Carry On Henry*. For once I was in the unlikely situation of being involved romantically with Charlie, as my character Queen Marie had turned off her sex-mad husband Henry VIII (Sid James) through her addiction to chewing garlic, and Sir Roger attempts to fill the vacancy: 'Didn't you know?' he proclaims before launching another attempt in the Queen's bedchamber. 'As the king's taster I have to try everything before he does.'

I loved *Carry On Henry*. Those gorgeous costumes and my French accent made it a real pleasure to act in. The same can't be said for *Carry On at Your Convenience. Carry On Abroad*, in which my character gloried under the name of Cora Flange, is memorable for the conditions in which it was shot. We started filming at Pinewood in April 1972, and we had hardly begun work on the outdoor shots before the wind started getting up. In a short time what felt like (and probably was) a force nine gale was battering the set so hard that the Mediterranean palm trees which should have been swaying gently in a light breeze were all blowing over. But *Carry On* crews were made of stern stuff and the filming schedule could not be affected by a little thing like the weather, so rather than abandon shooting for the day Gerry got a prop man to lie on the ground just out of shot and hold the palm trees down.

Charlie Hawtrey had a scene that called for him to be deluged by fire hoses, and despite the extreme cold he never flinched. One of my own close-ups had to be delayed: 'I'll have to put Joan under an arc light for a few minutes,' Alan Hume called across to Gerry Thomas. 'I can't shoot on her now – she's turned blue.'

*Carry On Matron* was made in more clement conditions. I was Mrs Tidey, whose baby is well overdue and who tries to induce the birth by stuffing her face with as much food as she can get down – not very medically correct but a good running gag for the film, as each time she thinks she's about to deliver it turns out to be another bout of indigestion.

During the filming of *Carry On Girls*, released in 1973, I again saw Sid James take a stand for what he considered proper behaviour. Two Members of Parliament were visiting Pinewood, and after lunch with Peter Rogers they came to watch the shooting. One of the MPs had clearly lunched a little too well and started making salacious suggestions to a couple of the actresses – in Sid's hearing. Sid was always very protective of all the *Carry On* team and would not put up with this sort of behaviour. He protested vehemently and demanded that they apologise. They did so – then made a hasty retreat.

*Carry On Dick* brought me a welcome return to period costume in the role of Madam Desirée, proprietor of the Birds of Paradise girl dancers, and in *Carry On Behind* I played Bernard Bresslaw's mother-in-law – even though I was only four years older than him! *Carry On England*, released in 1976, brought the series back to the army but is a film I'd rather forget. It had none of the magic of earlier *Carry On*s, and I loathed the costume: at that time I was putting on weight yet again, and it's not easy to disguise the extra pounds in an army uniform.

Weight had been a serious problem for me since I was about thirty, when I was warned by a doctor that unless I was very careful I would find it exceedingly difficult to keep the pounds off. I ignored his advice – but he turned out to be right; and, as my size increased, so my self-esteem declined. Oh, I tried every diet and fad you could think of, the most bizarre of which involved being injected in my bottom with the urine of pregnant mares. But in the long run I could never stop the needle rising on the scales, and have long since settled for being what might be described as 'comfortable'.

At the end of April 1976 I heard that Sid James had suffered a fatal heart attack while on stage in *The Mating Game* in Sunderland. He was sixty-two.

I had acted in seventeen *Carry On*s with Sid as well as numerous other films, and had worked with him on all sorts of projects – including singing a song as the Wicked Fairy in a record of *The Sleeping Beauty*, which was issued in 1970. The news of his death seemed to me to signal the end of an era. It also triggered a welter of stories in the press about the supposedly 'dark' side of his life. I presume that such stories increase newspapers' circulation (certainly the fact that they were so hurtful to Sid's family did not seem to register with the muck-rakers), but to me that sort of revelation was worse than distasteful – it was quite contrary to what I knew of him.

All my memories of Sid are good.

The papers said that he drank to excess, but I never once saw him drunk on the set – indeed, he usually went straight home after we'd finished a day's shooting, rather than hang around in the bar with other members of the cast. The papers said that he was a terrible womaniser, but I was never aware that he was. I didn't even know about the affair with Babs until long after it had started, as it began during the run of *Carry On London!*, a stage revue at the Victoria Palace Theatre in 1973 in which I took no part, being busy with other commitments. It was supposedly still going on when we were shooting *Carry On Dick*, but I can't remember anything untoward about the making of that film. I'm sorry if that sounds impossibly naïve, but it's the truth! (Maybe Barbara herself might have been a little bit more circumspect when revealing details of her relationship with Sid, but that's her business and not mine. I like to think that if it had been me, I'd have handled the situation in a different way, but it wasn't.) When the play *Cleo, Camping, Emmanuelle and Dick*, about Sid's supposedly lecherous and drunken lifestyle while making the *Carry On*s, was put on at the National Theatre in 1998 I made a point of not going to see it: I knew that it would have made my blood boil.

To me Sid was a complete gentleman, the ultimate pro and a great friend. I loved all the jokes and all the fun of working with him, and if just one memory of him remains with me it will be of him settling down to his poker school with Charlie and Bernie, and asking Norah: 'Got the necessary?'

By the time we made *Carry On Emmanuelle*, released in 1978, there was no denying that the series had run out of steam, and I have to admit that I considered that film let the rest of the series down. The inventiveness and cleverness of the scripts which had made films like *Cleo* or *Up the*

*Khyber* such a joy to work on seemed to have been replaced with a more smutty line of dialogue, which was no doubt a sign of the times but was not at all to my liking.

No one knew for sure that the series was on the verge of stopping, and Kenny Connor for one was confident that we'd all be back for another six weeks of merriment the following year; but the enthusiasm had gone, and I felt deep down that *Emmanuelle*, my twentieth *Carry On* in a row and twenty-fourth in all, would be my last.

As well as the films themselves, there were several spin-offs from the *Carry On* series. *That's Carry On*, a compilation of clips from the films fronted by Kenny Williams and Barbara Windsor, was released as a feature film in 1977, and there were no fewer than seventeen television programmes: Christmas specials in 1969, 1970, 1972 and 1973, followed by thirteen half-hour episodes of *Carry On Laughing* – with titles such as *The Prisoner of Spenda* or *Orgy and Bess* – screened in 1975.

During the filming of one episode of *Carry On Laughing* I was looking over Bernard Bresslaw's shoulder at the newspaper he was reading on the coach taking us to the studio at Elstree when my eye was caught by a photo of the ultra-hunky England cricket captain Tony Greig.

'Ooh, that Tony Greig, he's gorgeous,' I drooled. 'I could eat him on toast.'

'It's funny you should say that,' said Bernie, 'as lots of people say that I look very like Tony Greig.'

221

Now Bernie was one of the sweetest men I've ever worked with, but a Tony Greig lookalike he was not, and I raised my eyebrows.

'Are you sure?'

'Oh, yes, loads of people say I look just like Tony Greig. Look closely at my face – can't you see the resemblance?'

'Well, no, I'm sorry but I can't.'

'Oh, yes – people are always coming up to me and saying, "Can I have your autograph, Mr Greig?"'

Bernie continued in this vein until we had to start filming, and between takes he'd call over to me: 'Joan, look!' – and he'd go through the motion of bowling me a few balls. '*Now* can you see the resemblance . . .?'

All through the day he'd keep catching my eye and making a bowling or batting action, and by the time our day's filming was over I was exhausted through laughing at his antics.

The following morning I was in the rehearsal room at Elstree. I had not seen Bernie that day and had assumed that the joke had been forgotten. Just then the door opened and in walked this tall figure in cricket gear: white trousers, white shirt, cricket jersey, pads, bat, and even a little cricket cap perched on the top of his head. Not Tony Greig, but Bernie Bresslaw: '*NOW* do you see the resemblance, Joanie?'

That evening I rang Bernie's wife.

'Liz, do you know what your husband's been up to today?

'Do I? I've been up half the night letting out our son's cricket gear so that Bernie could get into it!'

The *Carry On* series had so dominated my film work during the late 1960s and early 1970s that, with plenty of television also on offer, I had little opportunity for other film roles.

There were a few, however. *Doctor in Trouble*, starring Leslie Phillips, was the last of the *Doctor* films and seemed to lack the comic quality of the earlier ones. This shortcoming was nothing to do with Leslie himself, who ever since the days of Miss Allcock and Mr Grigg in *Carry On Teacher* had been one of my favourite actors – very professional, and a million miles from his usual screen character of indefatigable lecher. I had a small part in *The Magnificent Seven Deadly Sins*, directed by Graham Stark, with a cast that included some of the great names of British comedy – Bruce Forsyth, Roy Hudd, Harry Secombe and Spike Milligan. In *The Alf Garnett Saga*, a big-screen version of *Till Death Us Do Part*, I was able to reprise my television role of the toothless Gran.

When I was offered a part in *Not Now, Darling*, the film version of a popular Ray Cooney stage farce, I was asked whether I could drive a Lambretta. I replied that since I could drive a car I could probably drive a scooter, and in any case I was assured that someone would show me exactly what to do, and they'd go round the block with me a couple of times before the actual shooting. I duly turned up on the set, was shown how to control the Lambretta, and the shot was set up.

Filming took place in a part of Chelsea where seven roads meet, and one camera was positioned very high above the scene to catch my riding up on the scooter. The assistant director gave me my instructions: wait over there in the distance on the Lambretta, and after the traffic had been stopped he'd wave his hand, which would be my signal to set off. I took up my position and gazed across to where the assistant was putting everyone else into position, and then I saw him wave in my direction. That was it – and I was off, puttering along on my little bike. After a few seconds I started to wonder why there was so much traffic swirling around me: this wasn't exactly going according to plan, and the more nervous I got the more tightly I grasped the handlebars of the scooter – with the result that it started accelerating. It was like something out of a Keystone Cops film, with me weaving in and out of the traffic, so gripped with panic that I had no idea how to stop the damned thing. When I saw a car coming straight for me I decided that it was time to bail out, so I wrenched the handlebars to one side, whizzed off the road and crashed into some park railings. A little stunned but otherwise none the worse for the experience, I picked myself up and staggered back towards the production team – and learned that the assistant director had not been waving at me at all, and that when I performed my ride the cameras had not been rolling.

So I had to go back, retrieve the scooter, and make my little ride all over again.

Second time round the traffic was stopped, and the cameras were going.

In the mid-1970s I was so much identified with *Carry On* films that I felt I was getting overlooked for other parts, and the offer from the Walt Disney Corporation of a part in *One of Our Dinosaurs is Missing* had me thinking, not for the first time in my career, 'This is it – this is the step up to the big time.' And, not for the first time in my career, that expectation turned out to be misguided; for *One of Our Dinosaurs* never quite made the impact that it should have.

It was, none the less, a wonderfully enjoyable film to make. Set in the 1920s, the plot revolved around a strip of secret microfilm which had been smuggled out of China (by Derek Nimmo) being hidden in a dinosaur skeleton in the Natural History Museum. The two main stars were Peter Ustinov and that wonderful American actress Helen Hayes, with many of the top British comic actors – Bernard Bresslaw, Roy Kinnear and Deryck Guyler – in support. Helen Hayes, Natasha Pyne and I played nannies, our role in the film culminating in a glorious car chase – or rather, lorry chase, as the nannies have nicked the dinosaur skeleton from under the noses of the Chinese nasties (led by Peter Ustinov) and, with Helen Hayes driving like a maniac, tear round the streets of London with the skeleton on the back of their truck.

Filming with Disney was a million miles from the cheap-and-cheerful mood of the *Carry On*s. Not only did I have a stand-in – dear Norah Holland, as usual – I also had a double (for action shots and stunts), and a car came to pick me up from home every morning and take me to the studio or to that day's location. Such trimmings apart, the big difference between making *Dinosaurs* and a *Carry On* was simple: time. For a *Carry On* we all worked our butts off for a short period (that was part of the excitement of making them), and with Gerry Thomas and Peter Rogers getting that creaky old machine cranked up and ready to go on day one there was a sort of adrenalin rush which kept us all going through those six madcap weeks. The Disney crew were not exactly casual, but there was much more a mood of steady progress, of having the luxury of taking time if that was what was needed. The mood was almost laid back.

Helen Hayes was a lovely lady and, for an actress with such a reputation, extraordinarily unassuming. She and Norah took to each other so much that after Helen had returned to the USA she asked Norah to go out to Hawaii and act as her stand-in for *Hawaii Five-O*. Helen also asked me to visit her at her place in Mexico, but as usual the old cold feet got the better of me and I never made that trip. (Typical! Norah gets the trip to Hawaii and Joan stays at home.)

Lunchtimes with Peter Ustinov were impossible. He was such a brilliant raconteur and such a funny man that the breaks were spent howling with laughter, and I could barely get my food down. He was also a tremendously gifted caricaturist, and I still have a copy of the sketch of me in my nanny's uniform which, unbeknown to me at the time, he made on the set of *Dinosaurs*.

Working with Tim Brooke-Taylor, Graeme Garden and Bill Oddie for a couple of episodes of *The Goodies* was also wonderful fun. The first occasion cast me as a hard-bitten American gangster pitted against June Whitfield in a struggle to rule the world of ballroom dancing (*The Goodies* always did go in for daft plots!), and in the second I played a nanny figure who is suddenly transformed into a power-mad despot. That second episode brought my one and only experience of the idiot board, and I wish I'd never gone anywhere near the damn thing. I had to deliver a long and complicated rant, and, try as I might, I just couldn't commit the words to memory. I confessed this to Bill Oddie, who suggested the idiot board; so, having strolled through the early part of my scene, I turned in the direction of the studio audience, focused on the board and started the speech. It was disastrous. The further I read, the more I seemed to be descending into gibberish. I had no feel for the words I was saying, and I completely lost my character. My voice got higher and higher, and by the end of the speech most of the cast and crew were laughing as uproariously as the audience. Audiences take a perverse pleasure from seeing an actor in difficulty, and the more my discomfort increased, the more they loved it. I stumbled my way to the end of the speech, but never resorted to the idiot board again.

Ronnie Barker, whom I had known since his very early days with Peter Eade, has always been one of my favourite actors, and during the 1970s I grabbed every opportunity I could to work with him on television, even playing a supporting role in the famous saga of 'The Phantom Raspberry Blower of Old London Town', which formed such a popular part of *The Two Ronnies*.

In *The Odd Job*, transmitted in 1971 as part of the series *Six Dates with Barker*, I played Kitty Harriman, whose husband (Ronnie) is suicidal after his wife leaves him and hires the odd-job man Clive to do away with him to spare him the bother of doing it himself. Clive was played by the then little-known David Jason, who stole the show with a marvellously well-observed performance. A couple of years later I played the daily in *One Man's Meat* in an episode of Ronnie's series *Seven of One*.

When I was asked to play opposite Ronnie in a new musical by Jimmy Gilbert called *Good Time Johnny*, set just after the First World War but based on *The Merry Wives of Windsor* (the Johnny of the title was Falstaff, played by Ronnie, and I was Queenie, the Mistress Quickly character), the prospect of a good stint in the West End beckoned. Before going to London the show was scheduled to play at Birmingham New Rep, but very early in the run there Ronnie – who was quite magnificent in his part – had to withdraw. He had been having problems with his voice, and it turned out that he had a growth on his vocal cords, a problem so serious that an immediate operation was essential. Ronnie has recorded how the night before the operation he sat in the bath in the hospital singing all his favourite songs as he thought he might never be able to sing them again, but mercifully he made a complete recovery and his voice suffered no lasting damage.

As far as *Good Time Johnny* was concerned, however, the loss of the star around whom the whole show revolved was a mortal blow. Ronnie's understudy John Baddeley stepped in and performed heroically, but a show which is a vehicle for one particular performer can never be right when that performer has gone, and in this case there was the added matter of Ronnie's physique. John Baddeley went on stage well padded, but padding is never a proper substitute for the real thing.

Unsurprisingly, the show never got to the West End.

While that was a blow in the long term, a more immediate concern for the Birmingham cast was to give poor Ronnie a little consolation for his having to quit. There were references to Krug champagne in the show, and although this was just before Christmas and Birmingham was teeming with shoppers, I took it upon myself to trudge the streets in the freezing cold and the rain and find a bottle we could send him. This turned out to be much harder than it sounds, but after fighting my way into and out of what felt like every supermarket and every off-licence in the city, I finally found what I was looking for, snapped up two bottles and began my triumphant return to the theatre. This involved descending into one of those gloomy pedestrian underpasses, and as I was passing the entrance to a gents' toilet in the depths of this tunnel an old wino emerged. He had not – how shall I put this politely? – quite finished adjusting his dress before leaving, and flashing his nasty at me he growled: 'Hallo, darling! You're a little cracker! Wanna come home with me?' I declined his invitation and hurried away. Talk about the perfect end to a perfect day . . .

Sitting on my mantelpiece as I write this are two little boxes which sum up my relationship with Ronnie – my Tit Boxes.

I was performing with Ronnie on television in *Before the Fringe*, the revue series in which we recreated various stage numbers, and one morning at the studio I was regaling the assembled company with an account of a wildlife programme I had heard on the radio the previous evening, in which an elderly military type was giving a talk on bird-watching. The old buffer's favourite birds were tits, and he described how he had built various 'tit boxes' and distributed them around his garden. There were different-sized boxes for different-sized tits: big tits, little tits, medium-sized tits. It was a completely serious programme, but his words, taken well out of context, were so funny that as I told the *Before the Fringe* team about this programme I couldn't stop laughing.

On that day I was wearing a shift dress, the upper part of which had two pockets with flaps. Having listened to my description of the old colonel's talk, Ronnie pointed to those pockets and suggested: 'I suppose those are your own little tit boxes, are they?'

A few weeks later the postman brought me a parcel which contained a small, brown, highly polished box which had originally contained the head for one of those old wind-up gramophones; engraved on the lid of this box were the letters TRESEP, the name of the makers of the gramophone head.

I was used to receiving strange presents from fans but this looked distinctly odd, and I opened the box warily. Inside, inserted in the round hole in the base of the box's lining and mounted on a bed of blue satin, was a ping-pong ball, with a tiny pink nipple made of potter's clay added to its peak. The accompanying letter is worth quoting in full:

TIT RESEARCH ESTABLISHMENT SOCIETY
EXPERIMENTAL PROJECT
(TRESEP)
Box House, Godalming, Surrey TB1 1TT

Dear Miss Sims
The members of the Society have great pleasure in awarding you this year's 'Tit-box' prize.

231

The prize is awarded annually to persons who, in the opinion of the Society, have done most to further the position of tits in our everyday lives. You have clearly demonstrated, over the past twelve months, that you care for tits, are concerned for their comfort and welfare, and furthermore have championed them in your work, thus bringing them to the attention of the public, indeed to the forefront of many people's awareness.

For your information, the Society was founded some years ago by the late Colonel George Slingsby-Martin, who first invented the Tit-box after spotting a pair of great tits in his back garden one summer. He said later: 'I realised I hadn't seen tits like that for several years; and all the nicer for being a pair rather than just one. Tits look better in pairs. It's more natural.'

So he decided to keep them together and invented the Tit-box, so that they would have a resting place. He made and distributed many such boxes all round his garden, and soon, each morning he would look out of his bedroom window and see them all over the lawn, and perched in trees.

Other people became fascinated by the sight of so many of these attractive creatures, and so the Tit Research Establishment Society was formed.

At this point we acknowledge gratefully that all finances for the Society are provided by

Berlei and Maidenform, who have offered firm and continual support for the many thousands of tits in our care.

We at TRESEP hope that you will treasure this award, and continue to champion tits of all sizes and colours, throughout the world.

R. W. Barker
Chairman, TRESEP Committee

A few months later another box arrived, containing another ping-pong ball (complete with nipple), this time painted gold, and this letter:

TIT RESEARCH ESTABLISHMENT SOCIETY
EXPERIMENTAL PROJECT
(TRESEP)
Box House, Godalming, Surrey TB1 1TT

Dear Miss Sims
We of the Society are especially pleased to be writing to you, as a previous Tit-box winner, to inform you that you have been awarded

THE GOLDEN TIT-BOX

This prestigious award is in the nature of a life-time achievement award, for your continual support and promotion of tits throughout your career.

This means that you now have two tits, and will be able to show them, as a pair, to all and sundry.

We at TRESEP wish you good luck with both your tits. They stand supreme, and long may they do so.

R. W. Barker
Chairman, TRESEP Committee

You stand supreme too, Ronnie, and long may *you* do so.

Another of the great comic actors with whom I loved working was Eric Sykes, and I was in several episodes of Eric's television series as Madge, who ran the bun shop. It is well known that Eric had a problem with his hearing which affected his balance, and he'd say to me: 'Come on, Joan, take my arm – everybody will think I'm pissed!'

One of the real stalwarts of Eric's television programmes – apart, of course, from dear Hattie – was Richard Wattis. I had done a television series called *Is This Your Problem?* with Dickie which involved the 'agony uncle' Godfrey Winn discussing viewers' personal problems, the nature of and then the recommended solution to which were enacted during the programme.

For one programme a viewer had written in to say she was thoroughly fed up with all the preparations for Christmas dinner and wanted a change. This was back in the days when television was shown live, and when Godfrey Winn, exceptionally nervous at appearing on the box, introduced this Yuletide story with the words, 'Now we're entering the season when you're all going to get out your wenny pistles . . . I'm so sorry, I mean penny whistles . . .', Dickie and I started cracking up. But we gritted our teeth and got ready for our scene.

Godfrey Winn's solution to the viewer's dilemma was that she and her husband should spend Christmas Day in a hotel – with the result that the opening shot of our scene had the camera focusing on a bowl of Brown Windsor soup, then panning out to reveal Dickie and me settling down to our Christmas lunch, Dickie in his best suit and me all done up in a mildly low-cut dress. Dickie was still suppressing his giggles while the camera was lingering over the soup, and I was just able to mouth, 'Shut up!' to him before we were in shot, though our hands were trembling as we tried to get a grip on ourselves.

Just as our trembling was coming under control, the waiter, played by Leo Franklyn (who had starred in many farces at the Whitehall Theatre), came on with the main course – Christmas lunch with all the trimmings. I was leaning over to finish my soup as Leo plonked down on to the table the bowl of Brussels sprouts, which he did so violently that one of the sprouts leapt into the air and came to land in my cleavage. Leo was not one to miss a gag if he could help it, and he started fishing down the front of my dress with his spoon to retrieve the rogue sprout. After a good deal of groping around he found the offending vegetable and put it back in the bowl.

Godfrey Winn's trouble with that spoonerism –

'wenny pistle' for 'penny whistle' – reminds me of a BBC producer named Bill Gates (no relation to the computer man) who, shortly after he joined the corporation, was summoned to meet the then Director General. Some of the other producers had warned him that the DG had something wrong with one of his hands, which put him into an even greater state of tension at the prospect of such a meeting, and by the time he was ushered into the DG's office he was a bag of nerves.

After chatting for a few minutes, the DG started asking Bill about another producer who had recently joined.

'Would you say that he's a man's man?'

'I don't know that much about him, sir,' replied the still extremely nervous Bill. 'But I do know that he doesn't smink or droke.'

'I beg your pardon?'

'I'm so sorry, sir. I'm frightfully nervous today – what I meant to say was that he doesn't smink or droke.'

Hoping to calm his young producer down, the DG took out a packet of cigarettes and offered Bill one, and as Bill leant forward to take it from the packet there was a terrible clash of heads.

Eventually this fraught interview was brought to an end, and Bill managed to escape without making an even odder impression on his boss. He subsequently learned that the DG had filed a note to the effect that this new young producer seemed a very nice fellow, but appeared to be rather hysterical . . .

* * *

*Love Among the Ruins*, a film made for television and broadcast in 1975, was directed by the great George Cukor and starred not one but two of the towering acting presences of the century: Laurence Olivier and Katharine Hepburn.

Katharine Hepburn really took me under her wing, and insisted that I be given the use of a caravan so that I did not have to stay in my costume all day long: between takes I'd go in there, take off my costume and relax. (This was a great contrast with the *Carry On* experience – not much chance to slip out of your costume and put your feet up there!) My particular recollection of her is her disapproval of smoking: on one occasion I asked her if she minded my smoking in her presence, and she replied in that famous drawl, 'No. I just feel sorry for you.'

The plot of *Love Among the Ruins* concerned a breach of promise suit brought against Katharine Hepburn by the scheming Leigh Lawson, and I played his hardly less scheming mother. My big moment was being cross-examined in court by Laurence Olivier, Katharine Hepburn's barrister (and dogged admirer), and I testify about how the supposedly engaged couple had been behaving in my house:

– . . . always whispering in corners and fondling and stroking one another.
–By 'fondling and stroking', I take it that you mean that sometimes Mrs Medlicote's hand might brush up against that of your son while they were

seated at the piano or –

–At the piano? Lord luv ya – they never needed no piano or any other instrument to start them fribbling and frolicking about.

Like most people who ever worked with him in his prime, I quickly fell under the spell of Laurence Olivier. It can be difficult to define exactly what distinguishes an exceptional actor, but there was no denying that he had a quite incredible charisma. It was fascinating to observe, however, that he suffered from nerves quite as much as the rest of us: the first time I ever met him, when the cast gathered for a read-through at the house Katharine Hepburn was renting in London, he was in such a butter-fingered state when he arrived that he promptly dropped the hundred pages of his script all over the floor.

Mine was a small role, but to be in the company of Olivier, Hepburn and Cukor made *Love Among the Ruins* one of the high points of my whole career.

# 8

# Low Spirits

By the end of the 1970s another stalwart of the *Carry On* team had died. In January 1979 Peter Butterworth was in his hotel room between performances of the pantomime *Aladdin* in Coventry when he collapsed with a heart attack. He had been in sixteen *Carry On* films and was always a lovely man to work with.

From my personal point of view, that spring brought even worse news.

One Thursday towards the end of April, Elsie Weedon, who had been Peter Eade's secretary at the very beginning of his career as an agent and who was running his office when I was first taken on to his books, came round to my flat unexpectedly. She did not beat about the bush: Peter had died of a heart attack the previous day. He had been complaining of chest pains late the previous week and had expected that a relaxed weekend tending the wonderful garden at his house in Hampshire would see him right, but after the weekend had mentioned to Laurena – who had taken over from Elsie as his secretary – that the pain was still there, and if anything was getting worse. On the Wednesday morning Peter phoned his doctor, who suggested a surgery visit that evening. Laurena went out to the chemist at lunchtime to buy some paracetamol, and on her return found Peter dead at his desk.

Peter, who was in his mid-fifties when he died, had meant a great deal to all his clients – Kenneth Williams and Ronnie Barker among them – and his death was one of the very worst blows of my whole life.

Professionally he had been the biggest influence on my career, discovering me at RADA and steering me through those early days in revue and rep; but as well being a wonderfully efficient and effective manager of my affairs, he had been a very close friend. He had taken me to first nights at the theatre and to the top restaurants. When my mother came up to stay in London he'd take us both out, which she loved, since he was an exceptionally kind and gentle man and I knew that every time she met him she was reassured that I was in good hands. I'd often gone to stay the weekend at Peter's house in the country, and we'd had many memorable foreign holidays together. I knew that life without him just could not be the same, and it was not until I joined my present agent Richard Hatton in 1996 that I really felt my career to be on course again.

The initial shock of his passing was followed by

the reality of life without Peter, and I soon discovered that I had little clue about how to manage my financial affairs: I'd left that all to him, and now I was an innocent abroad, swimming about aimlessly and trying to decide what to do next.

On Hattie's suggestion I contacted casting directors and asked for advice about finding a new agent, and before long I was signed up with London Management, with whom I stayed for seven years before moving to Mahoney Gretton.

But I decided I could no longer stay in Hurlingham Road. Sixteen years was long enough to live in one place, and with all the muggings nearby, the burglaries and attacks on my car, I was becoming more and more frightened of living there. The final straw came very late one night when I was turning out the lights downstairs before going to bed. As I was closing the curtains of the front room, I glanced out of the window. Hurlingham Road was deserted, except for one middle-aged man walking along the street.

As I looked towards him, three youths suddenly rushed up behind him, threw him to the ground and kicked him viciously; then they ran off. Horrified, I phoned the police, then rushed out to see if I could help the poor man. He was motionless and bleeding profusely from the back of his head, and I covered him with a coat as I waited for help to come. Thankfully, he survived; but to me this was a signal that the place had turned sour, and I needed to feel more protected. So although the housing market was depressed and I couldn't afford to buy anywhere else, I found a flat to rent near Kensington Square.

As usual I needed someone to take the bull by the horns as far as the actual moving was concerned – I had accumulated a large amount of clutter over the sixteen years and found the prospect of sorting through it all extremely daunting – and as usual the person who came and took charge was Hattie. For four days running she'd be driven over from her place in Earls Court by her son Robin, laden with armfuls of cigarettes and food for lunch, and we'd get down to business.

We started at the top of the house and worked our way down, getting every article of clothing out of the cupboards and wardrobes. Hattie would take each item individually: 'Now, darling, when did you last wear this? Are you ever going to wear it again?' – and then, depending on my answer, put it into one of the three bags we had placed on the floor. One bag was for keeps, one bag was for throwing out, and the third was 'Bruce's Bag' – Hattie's great friend Bruce Copp (who ran the Players' Theatre restaurant) was always collecting for charities. At twelve thirty prompt Hattie would call a halt and waft – oh yes, Hattie could waft – down the stairs like some elegant battleship, flurry into the kitchen and produce a superb lunch. Everything was duly sorted out, and on moving day Hattie supervised the whole operation. What would I have done without her?

I was soon to find out. Early in October 1980, Hattie died suddenly of a heart attack: she was only fifty-six.

Peter Rogers called her the Mother Superior of the Carry On family, but to me she was more like a Sister of Mercy. I've lost count of the number of times she scooped me up when I was down in the dumps, and her friendship, concern and advice had helped me through innumerable crises. At one point we were seriously hatching a plan to club together and buy a large house where we could live communally: what fun that might have been! Now she had gone, and she was irreplaceable.

Despite her serene outward appearance, Hattie had her own demons. She was paranoid about her weight, and although I managed to persuade her to come to Grayshott Hall with me once, she couldn't stand that sort of regime and gave up after a couple of days. Her private life, too, was very tortured. After her marriage to John Le Mesurier had come to an end she fell madly in love again – and when that relationship also foundered poor Hat went through a terrific amount of heartache: although she didn't exactly cry on my shoulder at the time I knew she was deeply wounded.

Her household had become like a second home to me, but at a price: looking on at the sheer normality of ordinary family life, seeing one or other of her sons popping in and out, would sometimes bring home to me acutely what my own life had lacked, and that feeling cut through me like a knife.

Hattie had been my greatest friend, and losing her was a terrible blow. Another was soon to follow with the loss of my mother. After suffering a series of strokes she had had to leave the house in Southchurch for a nursing home near where my Aunt Edith and her husband Malcolm lived; work commitments made it impossible for me to go and see her as often as I would have liked, and it was reassuring to know that I could depend on Edith and Malcolm to visit her regularly. But she was by now well into her eighties and her health started deteriorating rapidly. When the end was approaching, Pat Clayfield's husband Bill drove me down to see her, and she waited for me to arrive before closing her eyes.

Despite the occasional upsurge of friction there was a very deep bond between us, and I missed her dreadfully. I still do, and even all these years after her death find myself waking up in the morning and thinking, I must phone Mum and tell her about – and then with a sudden wrench I realise that I can't.

There was more to come. J. C. Wilson, who had been my accountant ever since I'd started out in the business and looked after all my financial affairs, died. He had been like a second father figure to me, and his death left another gaping void.

To have lost all these props of my life within a couple of years was crushing, and I simply could not cope.

At first I took refuge in drink. Getting too fond

of the bottle can be something of an occupational hazard in the acting profession; having been a late discoverer of the attractions of alcohol I had embraced it with enthusiasm, and it had been part of my life, on and off, for years – both a habit that got out of control and a refuge when things went wrong. On social occasions it was easy enough to limit the intake, but in the darker moments, alone at home, control was much more difficult to achieve. But whenever work was in the offing I would get a grip, since work has always given me the challenge and discipline necessary to provide a proper structure for life.

Some people said that it was my lovable rogue Tony Baird who taught me to drink. He had a Scotsman's love of whisky, and I tried to emulate both his taste and his intake – which in the latter case was something of a losing battle, since he could hold his drink much better than I could. From whisky I branched out to gin and tonic, dabbled in sherry, vodka and anything else that took my fancy, and later in life decided that a glass or two of Cuvée Napa would about hit the spot.

Drink became my friend, and although I'd try to control it, in times of loneliness – there was no partner with whom to share the joys, frustrations and trivia at the end of the day in my empty flat – I'd go on my own private little bender. As far as I was concerned at the time this was an entirely personal matter between me and my liver, but the press had other ideas.

During one of the periods when I had been off alcohol completely for a long while, I had tea at a London hotel with John Troke, who had looked after the publicity for the *Carry On* films and who had gone with me on the 'Viva Cartagena!' trip to South America. John mentioned how well I was looking. 'That's because I haven't had a drink for over six months,' I replied, and thought nothing more of it – until I was phoned the following Sunday morning and told to look at the centre spread of one of the tabloid newspapers. I went out and bought the paper, and there, beneath the headline MY BATTLE WITH THE BOOZE – BY CARRY ON STAR, was the story of Joan Sims's fight against the demon drink. That John Troke had been secretly recording our conversation over what I thought was merely an amiable tea together made me feel sick to the pit of my stomach, and desperately betrayed by someone I had known and trusted for so long. My mother was staying with me at the time and bore the initial brunt of my anger, but my friends all advised me to stay calm and try to shrug it off as just the way of the world and the sort of thing you have to put up with if you have even a modicum of fame. By the time of the follow-up story the next week – LONE-LINESS OF THE CARRY ON STAR – I was back on an even keel.

At some periods I would be drinking, at others not, but in any case drink can only ever paper over the cracks, and by 1982 I had got myself so far into the depths of depression that the inevitable breakdown could not be averted. My doctor suggested that I was worn out both physically and mentally and needed to go away and be looked after properly, so I was admitted to a hospital at Banstead in Surrey. This was the sort of place you went if you couldn't afford to be put away privately – while others might be able to afford The Priory, trust old Joanie to be banged up in Banstead!

I've been in some low dives in my time but had never seen anything to compare with that place. Over the years I'd got used to the sight of winos and vagrants shuffling up and down outside my house in Hurlingham Road, and now there I was joining them. For the first couple of weeks I was put in the assessment ward while they decided just how bonkers I was, and as I sat there, dark glasses masking my identity, I became enthralled by the old dear in the bed opposite me. She had been brought into the ward yelling at the top of her voice and smelling to high heaven, and after being deloused in a bath of antiseptic was tucked up in bed, from where over the next few weeks I was subjected day and night to a constant barrage of her foul-mouthed obscenities.

Then there was the German woman who scared the living daylights out of me by suddenly appearing as if from under the bed in the middle of the night and demanding, '*Zigarette? Zigarette?*'

While I was in Banstead news came through on the ward radio of the sinking of HMS *Sheffield* in the Falklands, and the idea that the country was at war shot through the ward like an electric current. Some patients went very quiet. Some started screaming. Some went and cowered against the walls. I was among very disturbed people, but it was none the less extremely weird to see a true feeling of terror take hold as a result of events that were taking place thousands of miles away and were no threat to us. There was a young man who hardly ever spoke but took quite a liking to me, and when that afternoon I was walking in the grounds he quietly came up alongside me and took my hand. Whether he was comforting me or I him I was not sure, but it was a touching moment.

After about two months I was discharged. I was glad to get out of the place, and it's not an episode on which I care to dwell.

To return to more cheerful matters . . .

I adored playing Molly Peglar in *Born and Bred*, a delightful sitcom written by Douglas Livingstone with a cast that included Max Wall, Gordon Kaye, Constance Chapman, Gillian Raine and Richard O'Callaghan. The story revolved around two families, the Tonsleys and the Benges, who are brought together when Annie Benge is awarded the British Empire Medal for her services to animals. Annie Benge, who lived in a house overrun by every sort of domestic animal that you could imagine (and a few that you couldn't), was played by Rose Hill, who was a very good actress but had one rather significant drawback as far as that particular role was concerned: she was terrified of all animals. For one scene she had to hold a rabbit in her arms and stroke it lovingly, which was clearly a great ordeal for her:

'How long do I have to do this for?' she called despairingly to the director.

'Only thirty seconds.'

'Oh my God! Thirty seconds is a lifetime!'

*Born and Bred* went through two series, in 1978 and 1980, and was very popular with the viewers. But for some unfathomable reason it was never extended into a third series.

A much more serious part – indeed, probably the most harrowing role I was ever called upon to play – was the Victorian child murderer Amelia Dyer, for an episode of the television series *The Lady Killers*, produced by Pieter Rogers (not to be confused with Peter Rogers) for Granada and broadcast in 1980. I've always been fascinated by crime and criminals (*Beyond Belief*, Emlyn Williams's chilling account of the Moors Murders, is one of the few books I've ever got to the end of without giving up), and I found Amelia Dyer a riveting character to play. Known as the Reading Baby Farmer, she was accused of murdering seven children who had been placed in her care (though she had probably done away with many more), and the play revolved around her trial and the attempts of the defence to prove that she was insane. They failed. She was found guilty and hanged at Newgate in 1896. This was a deeply disturbing role – a very far cry indeed from Belle or Zig-Zig – and as usual I hoped that it might help me shrug off the label of *Carry On* star and lead to more serious parts; but as usual it was not to be.

Equally far from the *Carry On*s, though in a rather zanier direction, was *The Cobblers of Umbridge*, a send-up of the long-running radio soap opera *The Archers* that was shown on BBC2 in May 1983. This crazy programme was written by John Fortune and John Wells (who each took several parts, alongside Roy Kinnear, Lance Percival, Willie Rushton and Derek Griffiths), and I had various roles which will sound vaguely familiar to anyone who, like me, is a long-standing *Archers* fan, including Lilian Beverly, Carol Begorrah and Norah Pepper. As Jill Cobbler I wake up one morning (resplendent in my curlers) next to John Fortune – my husband Phil – and we launch into a wicked pastiche of how *Archers* dialogue (at least in those days) always seemed to go:

–Morning, Phil!

–Morning, Jill! You know, I've been looking forward to this morning ever since last night.

–Go on.

–Yes, I've been looking forward to putting some of my pet theories into practice.

–About getting out of bed, you mean?

–Exactly, Jill. You see, according to this pamphlet produced by the Accident Prevention Research Council, it seems that it makes quite a considerable amount of difference which part of the body touches the floor first.

–Yes, I think I follow you. Go on! I'm with you so far.

–If it's the head, apparently . . .

–That touches the floor first, you mean . . .?

–That's it . . . quite a bit of nastyish brain damage can result.

–Point taken – but what's the alternative, Phil?

–Well, by and large the Council seems to recommend the feet.

–Always assuming, of course . . .

–Exactly, Jill – always assuming that the bedside rug has been firmly nailed to the floor!

–Yes, Phil, especially for the elderly and infirm. Our local branch of the WI have been trying to hammer that home for years.

–Yes, and quite right too, in my opinion. But it's not quite as simple as that. Even given the precautions that we've been mentioning, there's still a very real danger of a lumbar fracture.

–Mmmm – don't like the sound of that!

–Yes, and it's just as nasty as it sounds. Apparently –

– and then, mercifully, they are interrupted by the milkman knocking at the front door. Phil gets out of bed and plummets down a hole in the floor.

You'll get some idea of the sort of anarchic programme this was when I tell you that as Norah Pepper I get run over by a steamroller ('It fair knocked the wind out of me, y'see'), and that I supplied female dubbing for the part of Doris Cobbler, played (as was her husband Dan Cobbler) by Roy Kinnear.

Rather more orthodox than that barmy spoof were television appearances in *Waters of the Moon*, with Penelope Keith, and the Agatha Christie story *A Murder is Announced*, in which I was strangled with a piece of my own washing as I took it off the line. (I actually got to work with two Miss Marples: June Whitfield on radio and Joan Hickson on television.)

In *Deceptions*, a film made for television and transmitted in 1985, I played the housekeeper to Stefanie Powers' character. I'd been a huge fan of Stefanie in *Hart to Hart*, and the chance to work with her was one I grabbed with both hands. It was fascinating to observe how clued up she was about the technical side of film-making: she'd often go and stand behind the camera and help the director plan the shot. *Deceptions* also gave me the chance to act with Gina Lollobrigida, who may have been past the first flush of youth by then but was not a jot less stunning-looking than she had ever been: she remained one of the great Italian sex symbols.

*Farrington of the FO* was a television sitcom shown in 1986 and 1987 in which I first teamed up with Angela Thorne, who subsequently became a very dear friend. That series was fun to make, but by way of contrast I must confess that I hated my one and only appearance in *Doctor Who*. I was, of course, well aware that the programme had been a cult for decades, but it left me completely cold, and when in 1986 I was asked to play a character called Katryca in an episode, the title of that week's programme, 'The Mystery Planet', seemed entirely appropriate. The appeal of *Doctor Who* had always been a mystery to me. I didn't even know what the Tardis was, and it was only very recently that I found out that it was a police box: it could have been a letter box for all I knew. I'm sorry to offend the programme's millions of devotees, but for me an appearance in *Doctor Who* was simply a matter of learning the lines, going in, not bumping into the furniture, and collecting the cheque.

I had not worked on the stage for several years now, and it was even suggested to me that I had lost my nerve – that I could no longer face the ordeal of acting before a live audience and was dependent on the facility to re-record that went with filming. This was a good way from the truth. I'd long since felt more comfortable with film or television, not on account of any fear of the live stage but because the peculiar hours which the theatre demands – nothing to do all day, then having to stay up half the night to unwind after the performance – were becoming less and less congenial to me as I got older. None the less the criticism hurt, which is one reason why I accepted an invitation to play Fairy Sweetcorn in a pantomime of *Jack and the Beanstalk* at Richmond Theatre in 1984, with a cast including Keith Barron, Susan Maughan and Suzanne Danielle (who had played the title role in *Carry On Emmanuelle*). The panto did not cure me of my aversion to live theatre, but I had made my point.

253

In April 1988 came the devastating news that Kenneth Williams had died at the age of sixty-two.

Kenny had been a marvellous colleague. Apart from our twenty-one *Carry On* films together, we had worked on all sorts of other shows, from *A Tribute to Greatness* to *Stop Messing About* to *The Kenneth Williams Show*, and I had never felt more closely attuned to another performer than I did to Kenny. He had also, of course, been a very dear friend, and although I could not have gone along with his grotesque suggestion that we get married, we had many happy times together.

Sadness at Kenny's death was coloured by inevitable conjecture about the circumstances in which he died. He'd had problems with his stomach for years and had latterly been complaining of being in great pain, and when he had left his beloved mother Lou on his last evening alive he had told her that he'd take some painkillers and then go to bed: he'd see her again the following day. He was found dead the next morning.

There was no disputing that he had taken an overdose, but had he done so accidentally or deliberately? The coroner recorded an open verdict, but inevitably there was speculation.

I know no more about whether Kenny killed himself or not than anyone else who was closely associated with him. He was about to have quite a serious operation on his bowel, and I was aware that he was very frightened about going under the surgeon's knife. I also recalled that he had once said to me that he couldn't bear the thought of living to be very old. The simple answer to the question of whether or not he did away with himself is that I do not know, though I have to admit that I did wonder.

Six months after Kenny's death, Charlie Hawtrey passed away quietly at a nursing home in Sussex. He was seventy-three.

Yet another of the *Carry On* 'A' team had departed. We were becoming an endangered species.

But life went on, and there was plenty of work.

I've long believed that Victoria Wood is one of the very funniest female comedians we have ever seen, and it was delightful to work with her in 1989 on her television show – though I found it very inhibiting actually playing a scene with her, as I was uttering words which she herself had written and it made me excessively conscious of having to get the dialogue perfect.

In *On the Up*, beautifully written by my old friend Bob Larbey (who had been responsible for such classics as *Please Sir!* and *The Good Life*) and starring Dennis Waterman as a cockney lad who makes himself a millionaire, I finally got myself a catchphrase. 'Just the one' is the housekeeper Mrs Wembley's repeated claim as she pours herself yet another large sherry – and before I knew it I was being associated with that phrase: taxi drivers would let me into their cabs with 'Hello, Mrs Wembley – just the one today, is it?', and people would stop me in the street and announce, 'Just the one!' (I discovered later that I landed the part of Mrs Wembley at the suggestion of Bob Larbey's wife Trisha, who had been Head of Scripts at London Weekend.)

Derek Nimmo had long been one of my favourite actors from his roles in such series as *All Gas and Gaiters*, but he was also something of an entrepreneur, and one of his cleverest schemes was to take touring productions, featuring well-known British actors, to perform in the Middle East and Far East. Towards the end of 1990 Derek called me and asked if I'd like to join his company for a touring production of Alan Ayckbourn's *Bedroom Farce*. My husband was to be played by Peter Jones, with whom years before I had done a particularly silly television advert for Pom Pom sweets, the dialogue for which went something like:

–Pom pom pom pom pom?
–Pom – pom pom pom pom!

Alan Ayckbourn's lines were rather more appealing than that, and the idea of working with Peter again was very exciting. I'd just finished *Simon and the Witch*, a marvellous series for children's television in which I played a character named Lady Foulkes-Custard alongside Liz

Spriggs's witch. One afternoon Derek had been walking along Kensington High Street pondering whom he might cast in his Ayckbourn tour, and happened to glance into the window of a television shop. There, like some miraculous apparition, were twenty televisions, each showing Lady Foulkes-Custard in her full glory. Eureka! thought Derek, and phoned my agent as soon as he got home.

At first I was thrilled by such an offer, but then waves of that same old lack of self-confidence starting washing over me. I wasn't very keen on the flying which the trip would involve, and went through all sorts of ups and downs about it. I knew I should go, but I just couldn't face it, and sheepishly rang Derek to say I'd have to back out. He assured me that I was mad, that I'd have a wonderful time and that I should reconsider, but I was adamant – until just after putting the phone down I realised what a fool I was being. 'Joan,' I said to myself, 'get a grip on yourself. Go!'

So I phoned Derek straight back and said I'd changed my mind – and before I knew it I was in the rehearsal room in London.

Getting the play to a state of readiness was one thing. Getting myself to a similar state was quite another. I had to apply for a new passport, and was so flustered by all the bureaucracy involved that I managed to put the wrong century on the application form. But eventually that got sorted out, and by the evening before our departure all I had to do was pack.

*All I had to do?* I was all of a flutter and just couldn't get myself organised, rushing around my flat screaming and yelling, ordering taxis, trying to pack and generally getting myself into a terrible tizz.

In a panic I phoned Polly James, with whom I'd worked a good deal lately and who had become a great chum: 'You'll have to come over, Polly: I just can't get packed. And bring a suitcase!' She did, and I had to send her straight back to get a bigger one. It wasn't only my own clothes that I was packing: we had to take our costumes too, and mine was a heavily beaded number which seemed to weigh a ton and a half and took up far too much room in my luggage. I didn't think I was ever going to get on the plane; but somehow I got myself to the airport the following morning, and once the plane lifted off the ground and I was able to sit back and enjoy the company of the other actors, all my worries evaporated.

First stop was a huge four-star hotel in Dubai. Our performance took place on a stage constructed at one end of the hotel ballroom, and the audience had had a decent dinner by the time we came on at about nine thirty. (One day I was having lunch with Peter Jones in the hotel restaurant when I looked up from the table and there, on the other side of the restaurant, was Wally Douglas, who had directed several of the televised Brian Rix farces in which I had acted. His daughter now lived in Dubai, and he and his wife had happened to notice that I was in the play and were coming to see the show.)

We then moved on to Bahrain, Muscat, Al Ain (which turned out to be somewhere in the middle of the desert); then to Singapore and Kuala Lumpur before returning to the Middle East at Cairo, where I was able to visit the pyramids with Peter Jones and his wife. But even in such exotic parts of the world it was impossible to get rid of the *Carry On* connection, and after practically every performance people would come up and want to talk to me about Kenneth Williams or Barbara Windsor.

After Cairo came Djakarta and Jordan; the whole glorious trip lasted about two months before we had to return to the gloom of London in winter. It had been an amazing experience, the sort of trip I would never have been able to afford off my own bat, and although it was sad that work and travel had meant that we could not spend nearly enough time looking round, I returned hugely relieved that I had not given in to my inhibitions and wimped out of going.

I also acted with Peter Jones in *Tender Loving Care*, a black comedy by Lucy Gannon (who wrote *Soldier, Soldier*) which brought the chance to work with two of my favourite actresses in Dawn French and Rosemary Leach. When we were on location we were provided with a small make-up room, off which there was a small loo. This loo, though perfectly clean and neat, was very basically appointed – which brought out an unusual characteristic in Rosemary. It seemed that she had a thing about lavatories: they had to be properly furnished, and over the next few days she quietly brought in from outside the things which she thought would brighten up our little loo: curtains, a little rug, one of those little covers for the spare toilet roll . . . It brought out a whole side of Rosemary I'd never known about before!

As Del Boy's aunt in an episode of *Only Fools and Horses* I teamed up with David Jason for the first time since we'd acted together in that Ronnie Barker series, and I was delighted to be working with him again – and delighted for him that he'd come so far since those days. Filming that episode on location I got so cold that although I was all dolled up I had to wear wellington boots under my fancy costume – but then, after *Carry On Camping* and *Carry On Abroad* I was well used to such conditions . . .

It was back to Noël Coward for the role of the dour mother-in-law in a television version of *Fumed Oak*, one of a series of Coward playlets entitled *Tonight at 8.30* fronted by – and starring – Joan Collins, who introduced the play:

*Fumed Oak* is a black comedy of a failing commuter marriage. Henry Gow has worked in the same department store for years and is now a floor-walker. He goes to work punctually every morning, leaving his awful wife Doris, their awful daughter Elsie and his even more awful mother-in-law all moaning and wailing. He returns each evening to find them still moaning and wailing. Will it ever end . . .?

260

The play opens with a shot of that 'even more awful mother-in-law' doggedly knitting in the corner of the parlour – shades of Giles's old gran yet again.

Joan Collins herself played Mrs Gow, an uncharacteristically dowdy and unglamorous role for her – despite all the bitchy stories, she looked absolutely gorgeous without make-up – and Anthony Newley (who, of course, had been married to Joan) was Henry Gow. It was the first time I had worked with Tony since *Floggit's* a million years earlier.

The *Carry On* idea was not completely dead, and occasionally plans were floated to make another film. In 1987 there was talk of *Carry On Texas*, a parody of *Dallas*, and in 1988 of *Carry On Down Under* and then *Carry On Nursing*. The last-named actually got as far as the scheduling of production time at Pinewood, then the death of Kenneth Williams – who had provisionally agreed to take part – brought a halt to the project.

But one more *Carry On* film was made – *Carry On Columbus*, released in 1992, the five-hundredth anniversary of Columbus's discovery of America. Gerry Thomas rang me and asked me to play a part – 'A *Carry On* wouldn't be the same without you,' he insisted – but I had little enthusiasm for the idea, and was relieved to be able to tell him with complete honesty that other commitments – principally a new series of *On the Up* – made it impossible. I have to admit that when

261

I finally got to see *Carry On Columbus* on television I was pleased that I was not part of it: to me it was as if a whole new generation of comic actors were speaking a foreign language badly. It may have had the *Carry On* name, and it may have had Peter Rogers as executive producer and Gerry Thomas as director, but it bore little relation to the real traditions of the *Carry On* series.

In November 1993 Gerry Thomas died of a heart attack at his home in Buckinghamshire at the age of seventy-two. I can still hear him calling, 'Think warm, Joanie, think warm!' as we froze our way through *Carry On Camping*. Later the same month Kenny Connor died of cancer: he was seventy-seven. Bernard Bresslaw had also died in 1993, and Terry Scott, who had appeared in seven *Carry On*s, was to depart the following year. Endangered species? Near-extinction loomed.

The first series of *As Time Goes By*, written by Bob Larbey and starring Judi Dench and Geoffrey Palmer, was transmitted early in 1992. Yet again my character was named Madge, this time the rip-roaring, hard-driving wife of Rocky, played by Frank Middlemass (who, to make a tenuous link to *The Cobblers of Umbridge*, had played the last Dan Archer on the radio) – and with this part I finally started to shrug off the label of 'Carry On actress'. The series has become so hugely popular that people who stop me in the street now to say 'Excuse me, but aren't you . . .' are as likely to finish their sentence with ' . . . that lady in *As Time Goes By*?' as '. . . that person from the *Carry Ons*?'

The basic story of *As Time Goes By* is that Judi and Geoffrey, as Jean and Lionel, having been sweethearts before the war, meet up again and eventually marry. Rocky is Lionel's father, who woos and wins Madge – who might be old but adamantly refuses to admit it and insists on living life to the full. My first appearance in the series was quite wonderful, roaring up a country road in my huge pink Cadillac, stetson planted firmly on my head, whooping with delight.

Like all Bob Larbey's comedy, *As Time Goes By* gets its laughs from gentle, understated humour rather than in-your-face gag-making. Interestingly, the series has become immensely popular in the USA.

Acting regularly in a sitcom has a routine all of its own. The filmed sequences are made well in advance of the studio recording, which in the case of *As Time Goes By* takes place on a Friday. We are called in on the following day to read through next week's episode, then given Sunday off before returning to work on Monday, rehearsing each weekday morning and then recording in the studio on the Friday. On that day we first go through the episode very slowly with the cameras, blocking each actor's movements and lining up the shots. We run through the episode up to speed, more than once if necessary, and then do the dress run in costume. We then break for a meal before returning to the studio to perform the real thing in front of a live audience.

Working in front of a studio audience is wonderful fun, so long as you don't get inhibited if you make a mistake and have to redo the scene. Audiences seem to love it when that happens, provided that you don't take it too seriously. Let them in on the joke and they'll stay with you.

With a regular part in an established sitcom, life seemed rosy, and there was plenty of other work to get my teeth into. There was a cameo role in *My Good Friend* with George Cole and Richard Pearson, and a delicious part in *Pie in the Sky* with Richard Griffiths, in which I played one of a pair of elderly ladies who go round passing dud cheques. Then there was a television version of *The Canterville Ghost* with Patrick Stewart, Donald Sinden and Leslie Phillips, filmed in excruciatingly cold conditions; *Just William*; an appearance with Pat Routledge in *Hetty Wainthrop Investigates*; and some highly enjoyable radio, including a *Beachcomber* programme with Richard Ingrams, a radio version of the great Ealing film *Passport to Pimlico*, and a play called *The Two Sisters* with Robert Glenister and Barbara Jefford – the first time I had acted with her since we were at RADA together.

But in 1994 things took another downward turn.

I had a part in a television version of the Joanna Trollope novel *A Village Affair*. This had been a rushed production from the start, and the first day of filming on location in a wood near a village in Oxfordshire was very fraught, with too many retakes making the production people anxious about whether we'd be able to keep to the filming schedule. By the end of the afternoon watches were being tapped impatiently as we tried to make up lost time, and tempers were becoming frayed.

I had already done the major part of my first scene, with just my approach shot still to do. This involved my riding a bicycle through the woods towards the camera. It all seemed simple enough, but as I started to rehearse riding the bike, the front wheel hit something in the ground. The handlebars were wrenched round by the impact and, as I was thrown to the ground with considerable force, one of them was slammed hard into my ribs. At first I was just dazed, and a painkilling spray from the production nurse was enough to reduce the discomfort. Shooting was abandoned for the day and I went home to rest before resuming in the morning. I had a shower – which probably didn't help, as it must have washed away the painkilling spray – and went to bed, only to be awakened in the early hours by an excruciating pain in my ribs. The morning call was for seven o'clock, but by five I realised that I'd never make it. I phoned the production team, who suggested that when the driver came to pick me up I should get him to take me to the production doctor. The production doctor sent me off to the Lister Hospital in Pimlico for a X-ray. It turned out that

I'd fractured a rib, and would be out of action for weeks.

All sorts of attempts were made to juggle the schedule for *A Village Affair*, but in the end there was no alternative: I had to be replaced, and the part was taken by Rosalie Crutchley.

I was laid up at home for months, with little to do but contemplate the consequences of what had at first seemed a harmless little spill. Yet another opportunity to make my mark as a serious actress had gone by the board; and to top it all, I was also forced to withdraw from a children's science series for the BBC named *Cats' Eyes*, with the prospect of repeat fees for years to come. I'd allowed myself to think of that series as a nice little nest egg for my old age, and now it was gone.

Equity, the actors' union, was keen that I should claim compensation for the injury; a case was made, and for over two years it dragged on and on. I went back with my solicitor to try to find the offending root (or whatever it was), endless photographs of the patch of ground were taken, and once the two sides' lawyers locked horns I was subjected to a constant barrage of letters crammed with incomprehensible legal jargon. My greatest fear was of the case reaching court and my having to go into the witness box. It was one thing to be cross-examined by Laurence Olivier in *Love Among the Ruins*, quite another to go on oath myself, and the flippant remarks of some people – 'Pretend you're acting in an episode of *Crown Court*' – did not help. It may have been amusing to them, but for me the whole process was a nightmare, and it was with mixed feelings that I eventually took the advice of my lawyers and agreed to settle. The compensation I received was far less than I felt was justified by the circumstances, but it was proving impossible to gather firm evidence about what had caused the accident, and I was advised that legally we were on thin ice. So there was little alternative but to call it a day.

It was time for a fresh start. The mental anguish of the case had taken much longer to ease than the physical pain of the accident, and now I was determined to get back to work as soon as I could. My agents Mahoney Gretton had been wonderfully supportive throughout the case, but my determination to start again with a clean sheet made me decide to look for a new agent – and I was hugely fortunate to be recommended Richard Hatton. Like Peter Eade, Richard has always insisted on keeping his client list small but select, and like Peter he has become a very good friend as well as my agent. Under his guidance my career took on a distinct new lease of life.

By this time lavish costume drama on television was all the rage, and I got a great kick when I heard that I was up for the role of Mrs Gamp in *Martin Chuzzlewit*. In the event I was passed over for that part in favour of my dear friend Elizabeth Spriggs, but I had an excellent consolation prize in the shape of the role of Betsy Prig. In the event I was rather grateful to have the smaller involvement, as Mrs Gamp was a very big part with very peculiar phrasing and idiosyncratic constructions, and such a prospect, when I was still not fully recovered from my fall, could have turned out to be something of a nightmare.

Betsy Prig was hardly a glamorous role. The costume was little more than a bundle of rags, and the make-up people could really go to town on me: dirt under the fingernails, boils on the face, and plenty of yellow and black on the teeth. It was not exactly the sort of condition in which it was good to meet your public, but one afternoon while on location in King's Lynn, I was sitting in the caravan between takes when an old man walking past stopped and peered in the window. A few seconds later he opened the door and started talking to me. 'It's nice to see you in the flesh – I've seen all your *Carry Ons*', he began, and then he started rabbiting on about all the different films he'd seen. After a while I realised I had to get rid of him.

'I'm awfully sorry,' I said, 'but I do have to get on: I've got my lines to learn.'

'Of course, of course,' he apologised, and started making down the caravan steps – then came back up, stuck his head round the door to look at me again and said: 'Sad we have to get old, isn't it?'

The trauma of the legal case over *A Village Affair* had left me completely drained, but by the spring of 1997 I felt that I was at last on the mend – and just then disaster struck again.

It was the day of the general election, and I had

been getting ready to go to stay with Norah for a few days. I had gone out to vote earlier, leaving my suitcase in the hallway of my flat. Now, scurrying around to turn everything off before going away, I caught my foot on the corner of the suitcase and plunged forward, knocking my head against a chair. As I fell I heard my back crack.

There I was, prostrate on the floor, in agony, thinking: What am I to do? I was alone in the flat, I couldn't move and the phone was out of reach. I lay there for some time until I had got my breath back, then ever so slowly crawled on my stomach across to where the phone was and rang for an ambulance – and before I knew it I was in the A&E department of the Chelsea and Westminster Hospital. I'd fractured my spine.

Lying on your back for four weeks is not a very productive experience for an actress, and I was acutely aware that unless I could get up and get back to work I might easily be forgotten. This was a deeply upsetting time, and again depression reared its ugly head; but to detail the depths to which I sank during those dark days would be distinctly at odds with the title of this book. Suffice it to say that I got pretty low.

A step back towards normality came with an appearance on *Noel Edmonds' House Party* in November 1997. This was my first live television for years, and since there was a huge viewing audience I was frightened as hell – especially as I was being handed fresh bits of script just before I went on (which took me back to the old days of revue, with Peter Myers handing me new lines to keep the show topical). I went on as a sort of Fairy Queen figure, pranced around with Noel for a while, giggled, dried, then went off – but my mind is a total blank as far as details of the show are concerned. None the less, the appearance was a great boost to my confidence, and helped get me going again.

My conviction that things were getting better after the various traumas of the past few years gained strength when in the middle of December the script arrived for the television dramatisation of William Makepeace Thackeray's *Vanity Fair*. To learn that I was being considered for the part of Miss Crawley was wonderful news, and I was feeling extremely optimistic as I went to meet the director Mark Munden at Television Centre. He informed me that the last time he had met me was at Pinewood on the set of a *Carry On* film – he had been brought there by his mother, who was a continuity girl – which underlined my extreme old age (sixty-seven!) rather forcibly. But we got on very well, and as I made my way home my mood got ever more buoyant. Things were going my way, and I was about to raise my career on to a different plane.

It was not yet in the bag, however, and I knew that there were other people up for Miss Crawley; so the approach to Christmas was a nerve-racking time. I had hoped to hear news before the world shut down for the festivities – but none came, and at Norah's all Christmas I was trying to push out of my mind that nagging question: would I get the part or not?

I've never kept a proper journal, but I do still have my appointment diary for 1998. The entry for Monday 19 January reads: 'Didn't get part in *Vanity Fair*.'

...

# 9

# Blonde Bombshell on the Up

The disappointment over *Vanity Fair* hit me deeply, for a variety of reasons. I always felt very much at home performing costume drama; this would have been both a great part and a great opportunity to get into the front rank of – how to put it delicately? – the older actresses in these lush televised adaptations of the classics. Furthermore, it was clear that the part would not be particularly demanding physically, and since in the aftermath of the *Village Affair* fall I was not at my fittest or most athletic I had to be careful about the physical nature of roles I committed myself to playing. Last – but definitely not least – it would get me back to earning some serious money, and, not to put too fine a point on it, I was getting more than a little strapped for cash. I'd never expected to become wealthy from acting, but nor had I expected to end up on my own in a small rented flat. Something had gone wrong somewhere along the line.

With such thoughts nagging at me I started to

get things out of all proportion, and found myself wondering whether I'd ever get a decent part again.

But there was no time to sit around feeling sorry for myself: the rejection had scarcely begun to sink in when I learned that a close friend was in hospital with cancer. Although in due course she was to make a full recovery, the experience of visiting her pushed me back into the depths, and at the end of January 1998 I had to seek the help of a counsellor. This was a very chastening experience, not least on account of the lessons I was forced to learn, through bitter experience, about depression. Although attitudes are very slowly changing, it is still the case that the majority of people who have never suffered from depression simply cannot accept that it is an illness like any other – that it is caused by some trigger, and can be alleviated and cured through treatment. Just because you cannot see that the patient's leg is covered in an unsightly rash does not mean that they are not suffering from a treatable disease. There is nothing to be ashamed about in suffering from depression. It is perfectly curable – and in my case was in due course cured.

Alongside medication and counselling I was undergoing hydrotherapy for the recurring problems in my back and continuing treatment for alcohol dependency. In short, I was in a right old mess, and when later in 1998 I was asked to take part in a programme to mark the fortieth anniversary of the release of the first *Carry On* film, my initial response was to decline. The makers of the documentary had interviewed several of the actors – including Barbara Windsor, Jim Dale and June Whitfield – but over the years I'd tended to turn down offers to talk about the series as I was always keen to establish an acting identity for myself away from it. Another factor this time was that going to Pinewood for the interview would involve encountering the ghosts of so many of the team who had passed away: Sid James, Kenny Williams, Hattie Jacques, Kenny Connor, Charlie Hawtrey, Bernie Bresslaw, Terry Scott and Gerry Thomas had all died, and I was not sure that in my current state I wanted to be reminded too closely of the Grim Reaper.

But after a good deal of characteristic to-ing and fro-ing ('I'll do it . . . No, I won't . . . Yes, I will . . .') I eventually agreed to appear in the programme, and although the usual panic set in as the day approached – Would my hair look all right? Would I be able to give sensible answers to the questions? – it turned out to be a delightful experience. Peter Rogers and his assistant Audrey Skinner were waiting to meet me when I arrived, and Audrey, bless her, had fixed up a sign reading, 'Welcome home, Joan!' The ghosts were indeed lurking and the memories did come flooding back, but they were all very positive.

None the less, it was an inescapable truth that my generation of actors and film-makers was thinning out, and in January 1999 there was another funeral to attend: Betty Box, who had produced

*Doctor in the House* when my film career was just beginning to develop and was one of the legends of British cinema, died at the age of seventy-nine.

The following month I was sitting at home one Saturday afternoon answering the fan mail, which even at this advanced stage of my acting career still has the habit of piling up on the living-room floor – from all over the world, such has been the global reach of the *Carry On* phenomenon – and feeling, at least by my usual standards, on good terms with the world. Personally, I had recovered well from the last tumble and had been off the drink for over six months; professionally things were ticking along nicely, with a new series of *As Time Goes By* to be recorded and plenty of other parts in the offing. After a couple of hours of answering the mail I was ready for a break, so I made a cup of tea and lit a cigarette.

When I put the cigarette to my lips my mouth felt strange – a sort of numbness like you feel after being injected at the dentist. I picked up the cup to drink, and the tea started dribbling down my face. I did not think much about this curious sensation, and simply wiped my face, stubbed out my cigarette and carried on going through the mail. The rest of the day passed perfectly normally, but when the following morning I looked in the bathroom mirror, the whole of the left side of my face had collapsed: my left eye seemed to have slipped lower than the right, the left side of my mouth was gaping open, and all the muscle structure of that part of my face had gone. I looked hideous.

My first thought was that I'd had some sort of stroke; whatever it was, I knew that I had to get medical help straight away. It was Sunday morning and the doctor's surgery was closed, so I took myself off – yet again! – to the A&E department at the Chelsea and Westminster Hospital, where at first they thought it might be shingles (it was subsequently diagnosed as a Bell's palsy). They prescribed steroids and fitted me with an eye-patch so that I would not terrify innocent bystanders, and I went and found a cab to take me home to Kensington.

It was a short journey, but long enough for me to reflect. Just when life seemed to be picking up again, along had come another blow: there was not much chance of my getting a decent television part with a face like this, and how long would I be in that condition? Sod it, I thought, this really takes the biscuit – it's time for a drink. So I asked the cab driver to stop at the nearest off-licence and go in and get me two bottles of Cuvée Napa, my old favourite. When I got home I tucked in with a vengeance: I didn't get drunk, but I did sink deeper and deeper into that old reflective mood – and the more I reflected, the further down I went. I'd rarely felt so low.

After a few more days of quietly tippling and generally feeling sorry for myself, I contacted the counsellor who had been handling my case during my last bout of depression. I explained what had happened, and it was recommended that I be admitted to hospital so that I could be detoxed and properly looked after.

But then, when I was telephoned and told that a bed was ready for me, something deep inside me shouted out that enough was enough. I was sick of lurching from one crisis to the next, depending on others to rescue me when I slipped. Instead I was going to take charge of my own life and make a fresh start.

The first thing to take care of was the booze. Every drop of alcohol in the flat was dispatched down the kitchen sink, and I haven't touched any since. (My main tipple now is Diet Coca-Cola, which I consume by the gallon. Perhaps there'll be a huge headline in the tabloids: CARRY ON STAR ADMITS COKE HABIT.) Next I went to the drawer containing all those impenetrable legal letters referring to the case over the *Village Affair* accident, took them out and threw them on the fire. That felt like shoving a particularly unpleasant phase of my life down the waste-disposal unit, and it made me a great deal readier to face the world.

This change of attitude seemed to bring with it a change in my professional fortunes, and things started to pick up.

There was more work for radio in the shape of *Bookcases*, a comedy series about publishing – in which I played a tea lady – and a guest appearance on an episode of *Bristow* – in which I played a cleaning lady, alongside another of my old *Carry On* chums in the shapely shape of Liz Fraser. But the really big boost came when towards the end of 1999 I was offered a part in a new film for television.

*The Last of the Blonde Bombshells* is about the reuniting in the present day of a female dance band formed in 1944. Written by Alan Plater (who had written the script for *A Murder is Announced*), it is a heartwarming story, but the real attraction of *The Last of the Blonde Bombshells* was the sheer quality of its cast, which included Dame Judi Dench, Dame Cleo Laine, Sir Ian Holm (I like to keep the best company), June Whitfield, Billie Whitelaw, Olympia Dukakis and Leslie Caron. Talk about star-studded . . .

I play Betty, the band's pianist, and in one scene Judi (the saxophonist) and Ian (who had dressed up in drag in order to be the drummer) have tracked me down to the end of Hastings pier, where I'm playing piano in a bar. The location filming in Hastings was a hoot, since the pier itself had been condemned and seemed to be rotting before our very eyes. There was no loo on the pier, so when we needed to spend a penny we were forced to make use of the facility over the road, near the pier entrance. It was teeming with rain and my old back had been playing up, so every time I was caught short I was pushed from the end of the pier to the loo, all wrapped up in a mac with a rain bonnet on my head, in a wheelchair. I looked such a sight that had it been early November rather than December we'd have done a roaring trade asking for a penny for the guy.

That part in *Last of the Blonde Bombshells* turned out to be the best medicine I could possibly have been prescribed. It was as if the sun had suddenly come out to warm me just when the cold was eating into my bones. Twelve months earlier I'd been so low. An interview with me by Lester Middlehurst for the *Daily Mail* in late December 1998 painted a picture of a person in very dire straits, and there was nothing inaccurate about it. Now, a year later, everything in the garden was rosy again.

Which is not to say that my new mood of optimism has not been rigorously tested – and there's no better example of my ability to look on the bright side than a little incident early in 2000.

My friends Jack and Elsa Dean had invited me to spend a few days with them at their lovely house in deepest Sussex, not far from Hastings, and the day I arrived I felt in exceedingly – to resort again to that useful phrase – high spirits. The weather was glorious, a bright and sunny February morning with a chill in the air, and I had just finished the latest version of the ruddy autobiography I'd been working on over the last few months. It felt good to be alive.

While Jack took my case to my room I stepped outside on to the patio to admire the wonderful view of rolling hills and to breathe in a few lungfuls of that sweet East Sussex air. Deep breath, and –

WHAM!

One moment I was gazing at the rolling hills. Next moment all I could see was a huge expanse of cloudless sky.

I'd fallen straight off the edge of the patio and

was lying on my back, my top half on the grass and my bottom half wrapped around a bush. They say that the moment before you die all your previous life flashes before you, but now just one tiny sliver of my history came to mind: Kenny Williams, after I'd told him about the Mabel Temperley Prize for Grace and Charm of Movement, observing that it was pretty ironic, as 'you've spent most of your career falling on your arse!' Yet again, life was imitating art, and Joanie had taken another pratfall.

Even though I was lying there in agony and could not move, for some strange reason I instantly saw the funny side of this situation. The paramedics were at the scene very rapidly and offered me gas: 'Take several breaths,' they said, but I assured them that frankly I didn't want to breathe – I wanted to shout. And shout is just what I did, so that for about a minute the hills were alive with the sound of Joan Sims yelling her head off: 'Sod it! Blast it! Bugger it!' An odd way to react, no doubt, but it made me feel better.

Trust Joan to be an unorthodox casualty. When they decided it was all right to move me, they couldn't get the stretcher through the house; instead, they had to lift it over the garden wall and then, having ever so gently placed me on it, man-handle me back over the wall – which must have looked a very odd sight – and into the ambulance.

I had fractured my hip, and spent two weeks in the Conquest Hospital in Hastings, where I was niftily given a new one. One hospital ceiling looks very like another, and those two weeks on my back gave me the chance to reflect – not a bad idea in any case, with my seventieth birthday imminent, though I've never been a great one for intro-spection and soul-searching and it's a bit late to start now.

Acting has given me a freedom that I never really felt when I was just being myself: it may be a cliché of the profession, but I really do feel that I only truly exist when I'm performing. I've been like a sort of Walter Mitty, with the parts I play allowing me to escape from the reality of being a shy, unconfident, self-conscious person. Once I'm out there in front of a camera I've got all the con-fidence in the world, but switch that camera off and I sink back into my timid self.

Yet however much I've lacked self-confidence, I've had to fend for myself all my life – and I've done it. I'm the only one who's ever provided my bread and butter, and I managed to provide for my mother and father in their old age, so I can't have done too badly.

The fact is that I've never felt comfortable with the inevitable consequences of being well known, be they the sinister attentions of Mary Hennessy, the entirely harmless experience of being pinned to the wall and interrogated: 'That Sid James – what's he like?', or the burden of being a local celeb. At the height of the popularity of the *Carry On* films I was asked to open the garden fête at Laindon, and I had to make a speech. Somehow a simple 'Viva Cartagena!' hadn't seemed quite right for that occasion, and 'Viva Laindon!' doesn't have quite the same ring to it, so I asked Myles Rudge to write me a few words. I duly delivered these in front of the good people of Laindon – not the most hostile audience I've ever faced – and it turned out to be the most terrifying experience of my acting life. Never again, I vowed, never again.

Another occupational hazard for an actor is that so many people think that you are actually like the parts you play. One taxi driver, suffering no doubt from a surfeit of Zig-Zig, looked in his mirror and said to me:

'I bet you're a bit of a girl when you get going, eh?'

My retort was very prim: 'I don't know what you mean by that remark, I'm sure – pray keep your eyes on the road.'

(Another taxi driver once spent the entire journey talking to me about other *Carry On* stars – Kenny Williams, Kenny Connor, Bernie Bresslaw, Sid, Charlie – and came over all wistful; when at the end of the ride I got out, paid the fare and made towards my front door, he called after me: 'Shame you're all dead, isn't it?')

It's extraordinary to learn that anyone who is so minded can look up a website for Joan Sims on the Internet – if a little off-putting to be told that the bit of that site headed 'Trivia' contains just two entries. One refers to the video to promote the Morrissey record 'Ouija Board, Ouija Board' in which I took part in 1989 as a fortune-teller, and which was subsequently banned by the BBC (not on account of my performance, I hope). The other states baldly: 'Never Married'.

The last couple of years may have seen more lows than highs, but both my career and my spirits have taken on a new bounce with *The Last of the Blonde Bombshells* – a copybook example of my long-held view that whether you're up or you're down, there's only one way to react to whatever life throws at you.

Carry on.

# Index

# DON'T WALK IN THE LONG GRASS
## Tenniel Evans

### Introduction by Sir Alec Guinness

'THIS BOOK IS A DELIGHTFUL, SWIFT AND EASY READ: ALWAYS
VIVID, VERY OFTEN FUNNY AND SOMETIMES EXCITING'
Sir Alec Guinness

The first thing Aunt Edith did when she collected ten-
year-old Tenniel Evans from the London docks was to
take him to D.H. Evans and replace his lightweight
tropical outfit with English winter gear and woollen gloves.
It was November 1936. Ahead of him lay middle-class
life in a Midlands rectory with four unknown cousins.
Behind him was an unconventional childhood running
wild (and barefoot) with the *totos* amongst his hand-
to-mouth, tumbledown family, scratching a precarious
living on the fringes of Kenyan society.

It was the winning of a scholarship to Christ's Hospital
school that took him for ever from his halcyon youth at
Porgies – a mud-and-wattle bungalow facing the blue
hills of the Trans-Nzois – to Allesly Rectory, a big dark
house run by the wonderful, horse-faced Cousin Ailie.
In England he learned that life was extremely serious
and that chilblains itched just as much as tropical
jiggers. But he learned too that his second family at the
rectory was just as loving and idiosyncratic as the
parents and siblings he had left behind, and whom he
was not to see again for twenty years.

'THIS IS AN ENCHANTINGLY FUNNY AND NOSTALGIC
MEMOIR OF TWO UTTERLY VANISHED WORLDS, WRITTEN
WITH REAL LOVE AND FORBEARANCE'
Carla McKay, *Daily Mail*

0 552 99802 8

## BLACK SWAN

# A KENTISH LAD
## An Autobiography
### by Frank Muir

'Forget the Booker Prize shortlist. Here is something a lot more enjoyable'
John Carey, *Sunday Times*

'A treasure trove of funny stories . . . a warm, witty and extremely well-written book'
Sir Harry Secombe, *Express on Sunday*

For more than twenty-five years Frank Muir, in partnership with Denis Norden, produced some of the most sparkling and original comedy ever written for radio and television. Later, working at the BBC and then at London Weekend Television, he produced some of the most popular television comedy of the 1960s and 70s.

From his very first joke at the age of six, Frank Muir knew that his destiny was to make people laugh. He also knew from an early age that he wanted to write, but it took a childhood illness for him to discover that humour and writing could be combined. The death of his father forced him to leave school at the age of fourteen and work in a factory making carbon paper.

But it was during the Second World War, as an air photographer in the RAF, that he really began his career as scriptwriter and performer. At his demob in 1945 he moved naturally to London and the Windmill Theatre, before joining the BBC, the legendary partnership with Denis Norden, and half a century of fulfilling the boyhood ambition of that Kentish lad.

'This delightful memoir is guaranteed to put a smile on your face and leave you with the feeling that, while Frank is still around, life can't be all that bad'
Christopher Matthew, *Daily Mail*

'Warmth of heart, love of language, sense of mischief . . . he makes you rock with laughter'
David Hughes, *Mail on Sunday*

0 552 14137 2

# A PLAY ON WORDS
## by Deric Longden

A behind-the-scenes look at the filming of *Lost for Words*, the Emmy-award winning TV drama based on the Deric Longden classic.

In *A Play on Words*, Longden is at his wittiest chronicling the wondrous experience of seeing his autobiographical book *Lost for Words* come to life on film. Several years in the writing, his screen-adapted version of this sequel to *Wide Eyed and Legless* had finally been completed thanks to the continual needling of Dame Thora Hird, who breathed life into the role of his mother in both films.

In his own inimitable style, Deric describes the daily goings-on around the film set amidst the continuing chaos of his private world, where he serves as official guide dog to this blind wife, the writer Aileen Armitage, and as parent, therapist, chief entertainer and chef to their three and a half cats and assorted other animals. Despite the usual interruptions by this familiar cast of characters, his own brand of literary work somehow manages to get done.

0 552 14660 9

# MY MOVIE BUSINESS
## A Memoir
### John Irving

'IRVING HAS WRESTLED THE MOVIE BUSINESS TO THE
GROUND AND WON. NO SMALL ACHIEVEMENT'
*Los Angeles Times Book Review*

*'When I feel like being a director, I write a novel'*
John Irving

John Irving's memoir begins with his account of the
distinguished career and medical writings of the
novelist's grandfather Dr Frederick C. Irving, a
renowned obstetrician and gynaecologist, and includes
Mr Irving's incisive history of abortion politics in the
United States. But *My Movie Business* focuses primarily
on the thirteen years John Irving spent adapting his
novel *The Cider House Rules* for the screen – for four
different directors. The movie was nominated for seven
Oscars, winning two – for Best Adapted Screenplay for
John Irving and Best Supporting Actor for Michael Caine.

Mr Irving also writes about the failed effort to make his
first novel, *Setting Free the Bears*, into a movie; about
two of the films that were made from his novels (but
not from his screenplays), *The World According to
Garp* and *The Hotel New Hampshire*; about his slow
progress at shepherding his screenplay of *a Son of the
Circus* into production.

Not least, and in addition to its qualities as a memoir –
anecdotal, comic, affectionate and candid – *My Movie
Business* is an insightful essay on the essential differences
between writing a novel and writing a screenplay.

'A FASCINATING ACCOUNT BY THE AUTHOR OF HIS LONG
AND TORTUOUS PATH ADAPTING HIS NOVEL *THE CIDER
HOUSE RULES* FOR FILM' *Flicks*

0 552 99868 0

**BLACK SWAN**

# A SELECTED LIST OF NON-FICTION TITLES AVAILABLE FROM CORGI AND BLACK SWAN

| 99065 5 | THE PAST IS MYSELF | Christabel Bielenberg | £7.99 |
|---|---|---|---|
| 14493 2 | THE JIGSAW MAN | Paul Britton | £6.99 |
| 14093 7 | OUR KATE | Catherine Cookson | £5.99 |
| 13582 8 | THE GOD SQUAD | Paddy Doyle | £7.99 |
| 14239 5 | MY FEUDAL LORD | Tehmina Durrani | £5.99 |
| 99802 8 | DON'T WALK IN THE LONG GRASS | Tenniel Evans | £6.99 |
| 13928 9 | DAUGHTER OF PERSIA | Sattareh Farman Farmaian | £6.99 |
| 99858 3 | PERFUME FROM PROVENCE | Lady Fortescue | £6.99 |
| 12833 3 | THE HOUSE BY THE DVINA | Eugenie Fraser | £8.99 |
| 14185 2 | FINDING PEGGY: A GLASGOW CHILDHOOD | Meg Henderson | £6.99 |
| 14694 3 | VIEW FROM THE SUMMIT | Sir Edmund Hillary | £7.99 |
| 99744 7 | CHARLES: A BIOGRAPHY | Anthony Holden | £7.99 |
| 14164 X | EMPTY CRADLES | Margaret Humphreys | £6.99 |
| 99868 0 | MY MOVIE BUSINESS | John Irving | £6.99 |
| 14660 9 | A PLAY ON WORDS | Deric Longden | £5.99 |
| 14544 0 | FAMILY LIFE | Elisabeth Luard | £6.99 |
| 13356 6 | NOT WITHOUT MY DAUGHTER | Betty Mahmoody | £5.99 |
| 13953 X | SOME OTHER RAINBOW | John McCarthy & Jill Morrell | £6.99 |
| 14276 X | IMMEDIATE ACTION | Andy McNab | £5.99 |
| 14137 2 | A KENTISH LAD | Frank Muir | £7.99 |
| 14288 3 | BRIDGE ACROSS MY SORROWS | Christina Noble | £5.99 |
| 14607 2 | THE INFORMER | Sean O'Callaghan | £6.99 |
| 99803 6 | THINGS CAN ONLY GET BETTER | John O'Farrell | £6.99 |
| 14550 5 | PURPLE SECRET | John Röhl, Martin Warren, David Hunt | £7.99 |
| 14709 5 | THE YAMATO DYNASTY | Sterling and Peggy Seagrave | £7.99 |
| 99705 1 | SPEAKING FOR THEMSELVES: The Personal Letters of Winston and Clementine Churchill | Mary Soames ed. | £15.00 |
| 54654 2 | HIS BRIGHT LIGHT: The story of my son, Nick Traina | Danielle Steel | £5.99 |